Understanding Phonics and the Teaching of Reading

Understanding Phonics and the Teaching of Reading: Critical Perspectives

Edited by
Kathy Goouch and Andrew Lambirth

 Open University Press

Open University Press
McGraw-Hill Education
McGraw-Hill House
Shoppenhangers Road
Maidenhead
Berkshire
England
SL6 2QL

email: enquiries@openup.co.uk
world wide web: www.openup.co.uk

and Two Penn Plaza, New York, NY 10121-2289, USA

First published 2007

Copyright © Kathy Goouch and Andrew Lambirth 2007

A catalogue record of this book is available from the British Library

ISBN-13:   978033522226 (pb) 9780335222278 (hb)
ISBN-10:   0335222269 (pb) 0335220541 (hb)

Library of Congress Cataloguing-in-Publication Data
CIP data applied for

Typeset by BookEns Ltd, Royston, Herts.
Printed in Poland by Oz Graf S.A.
www.polskabook.pl

The McGraw·Hill Companies

Contents

Contributors

Myra Barrs was the Director and Co-Director of the Centre for Literacy in Primary Education in London from 1986 until 2004. Myra Barrs has published widely in all areas of the teaching and learning of literacy. This includes research into gender issues and the significance of children's literature for developing writing.

Teresa Cremin (previously Teresa Grainger) is a Professor of Education (Literacy) at the Open University. Her work involves research and consultancy around literature, literacy and creativity. Teresa is currently President of the United Kingdom Literacy Association and co-coordinator of the BERA Creativity SIG. She has published widely and is researching creative teaching and learning, teachers as language artists and learners as possibility thinkers.

Tricia David is Emeritus Professor of Education at Canterbury Christ Church University and Honorary Emeritus Professor of Early Childhood Education at the University of Sheffield. She has been involved in the field of Early Childhood Education and research for almost 40 years and considers herself blessed to have worked with international colleagues for much of that time, including participation as a rapporteur in the OECD's recent study of Early Childhood Education and Care in 20 countries. Perhaps Tricia's best known publications are *Under Five – Under-educated?* (1990, Open University Press) and the co-authored research review for *Birth to Three Matters* (DfES 2003, 2004).

Kathy Goouch is a Senior Lecturer at Canterbury Christ Church University. Her research interests are in play, children's early interactions and storying, and her published work has included early literacy research. She is currently researching the nature of interactions in baby rooms in nurseries.

Usha Goswami is Professor of Education at the University of Cambridge and a Fellow of St John's College, Cambridge. She is also Director of the Cambridge Centre for Neuroscience in Education. She has published over 80 peer-reviewed articles on reading and related topics, and she is on the editorial board of eight journals.

Kathy Hall is Professor of Education at the University College Cork. Her professional and research interests span literacy, learning and assessment. Publications include *Listening to Stephen Read: Multiple Perspectives on Literacy* (Open University Press, 2003), *Literacy and Schooling* (Ashgate, 2004), *Making Performative Assessment Work* (Open University Press, 2003, with Winifred Burke).

Andrew Lambirth is a Principal Lecturer in Education at Canterbury Christ Church University. He has published widely in the field of Primary English with special interests in children's literature, poetry, the teaching of writing, popular culture, politics and sociology. Andrew's books include *Planning Creative Literacy Lessons* (David Fulton, 2005), *Reflective Readers: Primary English* (Learning Matters, 2005).

Margaret Meek Spencer is Emeritus Reader at the Institute of Education in the University of London. She has written and published extensively about becoming literate. Many of her books are now among the classic works in the field of literacy. She continues to influence parents, teachers and academics around the world.

Patrick Shannon is a Professor of Education and Head of Elementary Education at Penn State University in the United States of America. His most recent book is *Reading Against Democracy* (Heinemann, 2007).

Acknowledgements

We would like to thank the parents (Julie, Andrew, Liz, Lisa, Matt, Louise and Marianne) and the teachers (Matthew, Helen, Janette, Ruth and Roger) for generously contributing their time and expertise. We would also like to thank Gillian for her painstaking transcriptions. Special thanks to all the delegates who contributed to the Canterbury 2006 conference on reading. Thanks to the team at Open University for their patience and help.

Introduction: sound and fury

Kathy Goouch and Andrew Lambirth

I would find it impossible to be engaged in a work of mechanically memorizing vowel sounds. Nor could I reduce learning to read and write merely to learning words, syllables, or letters, a process of teaching in which the teacher fills the supposedly empty heads of learners with his or her words. On the contrary, the student is the subject of the process of learning to read and write as an act of knowing and creating.

(Freire and Macedo 1987: 34)

The purpose of this book is to offer critical perspectives on contemporary education policy relating to the teaching of reading. The contention around the use of phonics in the teaching of reading continues to provoke passionate and, sometimes, *furious* responses from those for whom literacy education matters. For more than ten years, since the Ofsted report on 45 Inner London schools in 1996, national concerns about standards in children's reading performance have been headline news (Hall 2004). As a direct result of the furore created by Ofsted-driven media coverage of some contentious results and interpretations (see Hall 2004 for full analysis), central government were able to prescribe both subject content and pedagogy by introducing the National Literacy Strategy in 1998. Each day and term's literacy hour for each age group in primary schools was then scripted by lists of objectives. This political management of teachers' roles and responsibilities in relation to the teaching of English had enormous historic importance, not least because it was non-statutory guidance and yet, as it was driven by Ofsted, it was almost universally adopted. It is important to note that all literacy requirements were, and still are, directed solely at schools in England and not the rest of the United Kingdom, where education authorities have different curriculum arrangements, different assessment require-ments and different reporting opportunities.

Although the National Literacy Strategy emphasized a 'searchlights' model and acknowledged the importance of all strategies used by readers, there was still a huge amount of guidance relating to phonics teaching (DfEE 1999) and this continued to be a central element to the Strategy's instructions to teachers and Ofsted's reporting of the teaching of reading (Lewis and Ellis 2006).

Other English-speaking countries were taking similar routes. In common with the Review of the Teaching of Early Reading (2006) carried out in England, in the United States the National Reading Panel reported in 2000 and in Australia the National Enquiry into the Teaching of Literacy published a report in 2005. Each of the three countries reported research findings leading to the recommendation of systematic teaching of synthetic phonics in the early stages of education. Each also issued similar statements regarding the initiation and the nature of their research; that is, they were all initiated in part by the concerns of psychologists, and findings were based on 'rigorous, evidence based research' (NETL) and 'scientifically based reading research' (NRP). In the report of the National Reading Panel claims for 'scientific research' and 'scientifically based reading programs' are frequently made.

The apparent political panic about reading standards, represented by these three reports, is associated with a particular group of lobbyists, and is in spite of the fact that in England, in 2005, 87 per cent of girls and 82 per cent of boys (Hall 2006) had achieved a nominated 'level', Level 4, in Standard Attainment Tasks undertaken by all children in English classrooms. There is, also, though a more seductive argument for some concerns about reading and that is the so-called, 'long tail of under-achievement', an unpleasant phrase used by politicians and policy makers to describe a group of young children who are considered to have failed if they were unable to meet predetermined standards at predetermined stages of their early schooling. Unsurprisingly, it seems that the majority of the children in this group are from low-income families (Solity 2006).

For some, the way to resolve this has been to offer, instead of an enriched layer of literacy experience, 'a thinner gruel of educational nourishment' (Meek 1987: viii). Although Meek argues that this kind of 'basic' or 'functional' approach to teaching reading is 'a particular kind of insult', others argue that it has a deeper significance in its impact on young children and this argument is worthy of the inclusion of a lengthy quotation:

> Some longitudinal studies have shown us that children provided
> with predominantly direct or 'programmed' instruction some-
> times do better academically than those provided with other

forms of pedagogy in the short term. But the studies also suggest that, when apparent, these gains are short-lived, with all significant differences having 'washed out' within a year of the provision ending. Highly structured, didactic teaching has also been found to result in young children showing significantly increased stress/anxiety behaviour (Burts et al. 1990). A longitudinal and rigorous study conducted by Schweinhart and Weikart (1997) showed little difference in the academic performance of young children provided exclusively with direct instruction, but they did find significantly more emotional impairment and disturbance leading to greater need for special educational provision.

(Siraj-Blatchford and Sylva 2004: 725)

Any system that jeopardizes young children's well-being must be questioned, loudly and persistently, by all those concerned with educational practices and a political system which legitimizes 'rhetoric and lobbying' as 'the basis on which decisions about teaching come to be made' (Hall 2006: 20) must be particularly challenged.

As a response, then, to the review of reading commissioned by the then Secretary of State for Education, Ruth Kelly, in June 2005, on 6 January 2006 more than two hundred and fifty people gathered together in a university lecture theatre in Canterbury and spent the entire day listening to, puzzling about and challenging ideas about how young children learn to read. The interim report from the Review was published in December 2005, in time for contributors to weave their knowledge of the interim findings into their conference participation.

The Canterbury conference was an opportunity for teachers and advisers to join with academics to interpret research findings and to sharpen their understanding of what it meant to teach children to read. The community of learners attending and addressing the conference sought more than a narrow official policy line and reductionist definitions of 'teaching' and 'reading'; instead they were keen to hear about research findings from informed researchers and take part in professional conversations with informed professionals. The conference venue would not hold more than this number of people and many requests for places had to be refused. Perhaps we should have followed our initial instincts to hold a rally in Trafalgar Square; the passion, concern and commitment evident at the time would certainly have supported it! Since that day there appears to have been little overt public resistance to the centrally driven requirement to adopt a single approach of synthetic phonics, dramatically changing both the content and method of teaching reading to young children.

And so in this book we make no apologies for offering oppositional responses to these current trends in the policies relating to the teaching of reading of English-speaking countries. Ultimately, it is only children themselves who will reap the rewards, or otherwise, of our decisions about their education. Let's hope that they are being made with the interests of children in mind. We are attempting to address the 'deafening silence' of opposition to current policy in relation to the teaching of reading and have gathered together a group of concerned individuals, including those who addressed the conference, to voice alternative visions and offer informed views about the teaching of reading.

The authors in this book have responded to contemporary policy for the teaching of reading in multiple ways, utilizing research and practice to make their arguments differently. The authors hope to contribute to readers' understanding of both the macro- and micro-processes behind the teaching of phonics and the teaching of reading through these diverse paths. In doing so, clear themes emerge. These include reminders that the teaching and learning of reading are human processes, subject to the uncertainties and unpredictability that comes with operating within the socio-cultural diversity of human kind. Many of the authors allude directly or indirectly to the current culture of positivism in educational policy for reading with its focus on objectivity, efficiency and technique. Advocates of this form of rationalization fail to understand or try to consider how positivism also has a connection with the untidy world of beliefs and values. With this approach to forming educational policy comes what might be described as the suppression of historical consciousness (Giroux 1997) and the ability to critically examine policy using the tools of history. In the first chapter of this book Tricia David discusses what early childhood is for. In so doing, she appeals to a historical consciousness to understand the changing nature of the perceptions and conceptions of early childhood experience and adult expectations for the trajectories of children's growth and maturation. These expectations include the way children learn to be literate and begin to read. In addition to a historical consciousness, Tricia David describes some of the research which shows how cultural expectations found in different parts of the world also play a role in a society's methods of teaching and learning reading and writing. The present focus upon early reading in school makes Tricia David's chapter on the functions of early childhood an insightful start to this book and to a reader's understanding of phonics and the teaching of reading.

The perceptions and expectations of children in a society which Professor David discusses are contrasted with an understanding of how parents themselves perceive their own children's development as readers. Chapter 2 provides an insight into the thoughts of parents of children who have just started, or are about to begin school. It is the first of two chapters that present conversations with parents and practitioners. Each of these chapters offer the perspectives of those who are physically and emotionally the closest to young children; in doing so we hope to highlight the physical, messy and emotional human contact that these people have with children. We want to reinforce how care is central to what they do and contrast the nature of these human relationships with the technocratic rationality that permeates much of the current policy for the teaching of reading. In each of these discussion chapters we present a commentary on what the groups say. Chapter 2 presents a group of parents informally discussing their own children's first experiences with reading the written word. Interestingly, the perspectives on children's development coincide in many ways with that provided by the teachers in Chapter 6. A theme that recurs in both of these chapters (but that can also be found across a number of other chapters in this book) is the importance of pleasure, meaning and relevance in learning, which in turn are related to the cultures of the children discussed. The parents describe how their children have found books 'to hand' and utilize them for their fun and individual affordances. They become the centre of many social and loving encounters with parents and siblings. This chapter and that of the teachers have become central to the whole book, as the participants present unique perspectives that act as living illustrations of much of what is said about learning to read across the contents of the book. In discussing and comparing their own understanding of how children learn to read the parents in Chapter 2 assist our own understanding of the how readers develop – with or without phonics.

Kathy Goouch has concentrated specifically upon the early years of literacy. She confronts, head on, contemporary policy and advice on the teaching of reading that uses one method – namely synthetic phonics. The chapter contrasts these methods with a case study of a pre-school child meeting print for the first time and argues for more 'organic connections' to be made between school literacy experiences and those of the home. Kathy Goouch describes the discourse of schooled literacy and its control and suppression over the possibilities of alternative practice and presents a vision of what could be.

Patrick Shannon describes policies for reading in the United States of America. This chapter provides the means for readers around the world to compare their own government's policies for reading with those of the USA and begin to understand their origins and the political and, sometimes, commercial interests of their advocates. Patrick Shannon demonstrates how sources of expertise and authority in the study of reading and reading instruction have been squeezed to exclude nearly everyone but those working in the field of psychology. As policy makers attempt to rationalize reading instruction, diverse definitions and values concerning reading have been excluded from the debate. This includes the knowledge of experienced teachers and educationalists. Yet, as Professor Shannon points out, it is those who have most contact with children and teaching and learning in schools whose perspectives still present the most powerful model of how to teach reading.

Patrick Shannon's work is complemented by the voices of teachers in the following chapter. Here, teachers from England describe their own understanding of how children learn to read. Their comments provide a powerful commentary on the current issues on the teaching of reading facing many around the world. For those teaching the very youngest children, current ideas advocating blanket single methods for the teaching of reading are considered an anathema to everything these teachers know about young learners and how teachers, as professionals, apply their own pedagogical craft. Strong messages arise from this chapter concerning pedagogy and the pressures applied to children and teachers about expectations and the judgements of standards and achievement. Again and again, we found ourselves returning to what these teachers were saying. They represented a central core to other messages coming from the authors in this book.

Kathy Hall uses Wenger's complex but enlightening notion of the interplay between reification and participation to cleave open the processes at work in our classrooms. In doing so Professor Hall presents us with a powerful analytical framework with which to examine contemporary preoccupations with phonics prescription. This is an absorbing chapter which will nourish readers with new and challenging insights.

Andrew Lambirth continues the theme of learning to read as a cultural process. In this chapter he uses the later work of Basil Bernstein to analyse the pedagogies that lie behind different traditions of the teaching of reading. Using Bernstein's conceptual framework that describes pedagogy as a form of cultural relay he shows how economic and social inequalities in the wider society are reflected in inequalities of success in reading and in education more generally. Avoiding a purely deterministic approach, he shows how the pedagogies of reading – those that are linked to both traditional and progressive models – contain social class assumptions which undermine the progress of children from the working class. He argues for progressive educators to understand the macro-processes at work within learning institutions and practise their craft as a means for political change to create opportunities for equality in education and the wider society.

Usha Goswami provides an argument for children to be encouraged to use a range of strategies to read. Professor Goswami has an esteemed background in research in the field of psychology. She offers rigorous research-backed arguments that question single-method approaches to the teaching of reading. She draws on a positivist research paradigm to make her powerful arguments and provides a distinctive response to contemporary policy for the teaching of reading. She provides tangible evidence for questioning the use of single methods to teach reading and therefore contributes to an understanding of the connections between phonics knowledge and successful reading.

Chapter 9 offers readers the opportunity to hear the conversations between two of the best known and respected teachers and scholars of literacy in the United Kingdom. In this chapter Myra Barrs and Margaret Meek Spencer begin, in conversation, describing their introduction to Chittenden, Salinger and Bussis's book *Inquiry into Meaning*. This book is now available in a revised edition (2001). The chapter provides both Myra Barrs's and Margaret Meek Spencer's perspectives on the importance of this book and the longitudinal study it presents. The chapter ends with their musings on contemporary reading policy's reductive approach to the processes and strategies employed by readers. Margaret and Myra contrast the limitations of traditional scientific paradigms to understand the processes of reading with the rigorous analysis of qualitative data found in *Inquiry into Meaning* and lament how this latter form of research is sidelined by policy makers.

The final chapter by Teresa Cremin argues for the pleasure and joy of reading to be a central part of learning to be a reader. It presents a picture of hope and inspiration for all those concerned to encourage children to want to read and to *feel* like reading and finishes the book on a powerful note of optimism for the future.

By the end of this book we hope that readers will, through a deeper understanding of the micro- and macro-processes involved in contemporary reading policy and its accompanying methods, feel more confident to challenge ill thought out and poorly judged approaches to the teaching of reading. The teaching of reading is too important and too serious a matter to allow us to adopt a passive approach, or look for a balanced or compromised response. We hope this book will sharpen the resolve of parents, professionals and academics to ensure that children are treated, in all educational settings, as unique human beings deserving of a rich introduction to reading.

References

Chittenden, E., Salinger, T. with Bussis, A.M. (2001) *Inquiry into Meaning: An Investigation of Learning to Read*, revised edition with an introduction by Deborah Meier. New York: Teachers' College Press.

DEST (2005) *Teaching Reading: Report and Recommendations*. Canberra: Commonwealth of Australia.

DfEE (1998) *The National Literacy Strategy: A Framework for Teaching*. London: DfEE.

DfEE (1999) *Progression in Phonics*. London: DfEE.

Freire, P. and Macedo, D. (1987) *Literacy: Reading the Word and the World*. London: Routledge.

Giroux, H. (1997) *Pedagogy and the Politics of Hope: Theory, Culture, and Schooling*. Oxford: Westview.

Hall, K. (2004) *Literacy and Schooling: Towards Renewal in Primary Education Policy*. Aldershot: Ashgate.

Hall, K. (2006) How children learn to read and how phonics helps, in M. Lewis and S. Ellis, *Phonics Practice, Research and Policy*. London: Paul Chapman Publishing.

Lewis, M. and Ellis, S. (2006) *Phonics Practice, Research and Policy*. London: Paul Chapman Publishing.

Meek, M. (1987) Foreword, in P. Freire and D. Macedo, *Literacy: Reading the Word and the World*. London: Routledge.

National Reading Panel (2000) *Teaching Children to Read: An Evidence-based Assessment of the Scientific Research Literature on Reading and its Implications for Reading Instruction*. Washington, DC: NICHD.

Office for Standards in Education (1996) *The Teaching of Reading in 45 Inner London Primary Schools: A Report of Her Majesty's Inspectors in Collaboration with the LEAs of Islington, Southwark and Tower Hamlets*. London: Crown Copyright.

Rose, J. (2006) *An Independent Review of the Teaching of Early Reading*. London: DfES.

Siraj-Blatchford, I. and Sylva, K. (2004) Researching pedagogy in English pre-schools, *British Educational Research Journal*, 30 (5), October: 713–30.

Solity, (2006) An instructional perspective on the Rose Review, in M. Lewis and S. Ellis (eds) *Phonics: Practice, Research and Policy*. London: UKLA/PCP.

1 What is early childhood for?

Tricia David

Introduction

In this chapter I want to explore ideas about early childhood, what it is considered to be 'for' in the UK today and what babies and children need to experience in order to engage in early literacy activities. First, I will explore what is meant by 'early childhood' and what happens, particularly in relation to brain development, during the earliest phase of life.

What do we mean by early childhood?

The period from birth to eight years was the traditional, international definition of early childhood. This can be seen in the Jesuits' maxim, 'Give me a child until he is seven and I will give you the man' – meaning that these are the years in which the future beliefs and attitudes of a human being are shaped through experience.

In the UK, the legal requirement, made statutory over a hundred years ago, that children be admitted to school following their fifth birthday[1] has meant that, despite most other European countries admitting children to school at age 6 or 7, the designation 'early childhood' has tended to be used to mean birth to 5. Some educationists and early childhood specialists, such as the McMillan sisters in the early part of the twentieth century, Belle Tutaev, founder of the voluntary playgroup/pre-school movement in the 1960s, and members of OMEP (*l'Organization Mondiale pour l'Education Préscolaire*), continued to call for changes that would acknowledge birth to 7 as a more appropriate period to recognize as a stage in life requiring appropriate and coherent planning and provision. This is not to say such planning and provision should not take account of different developmental stages within that phase; on the contrary, the complexity of children's development and the astounding rate of learning during this phase might be thought to demand even higher levels of expertise and competence from practitioners than that required for work with older children. Perhaps we can assume from their maxim that the Jesuits would have endorsed this view.

What happens in early childhood?

It has only been during the last quarter of a century that scientific knowledge about the development of babies and young children has begun to demonstrate the amazing abilities they possess and build upon. Although parents, grandparents, carers and even the children themselves later in life may have noted these abilities throughout centuries, attitudes to young children and the insistence on scientific methods akin to those used in physics and chemistry in psychology laboratories in the early years of the discipline's academic existence led, under-standably, to gross underestimation of young children's powers.

The physical immaturity of babies was misinterpreted as signifying a total lack of ability in all aspects of human life. Further, maturation theories led to misunderstandings about development so that the influence of nature (the abilities one is born with, inherited from ancestors) was accorded precedence over nurture (what one gains from experience). Subsequently nurture began to be seen as the more important of the two, with scant attention being paid to intra-child characteristics. Now the two are acknowledged as synergistic and interdependent. So not only do we know that babies come into the world 'programmed' to be social, to want to interact with other human beings and innately curious about the world around them, they can within a few hours of birth, for example, distinguish between the language/s upon which they have been eavesdropping during gestation and those with which they are unfamiliar. Within roughly the first two years of life most have become not only independently mobile and able to control head and eye movements, they are such keen observers of family members that they are able to 'mind-read' – to know what makes one of their familiar others happy, sad, angry, loving, and so on.

These new ways of thinking about brain development in babies and young children are neatly summed up in Figure 1.1.

The main implication of this new understanding and new knowledge about how young children think and learn is that we need to consider very carefully what we want them to be capable of and able to achieve during this period of life – and what they themselves prioritize as important.

What we used to believe	What research seems to indicate
Brain development depends on the genes you inherit.	Brain development occurs as a result of a complex interweaving of one's genetic potential and experiences.
Experiences before the age of three do not influence later development very much.	Early experiences affect the 'design' of the brain, and influence the nature and extent of adult capabilities.
A secure relationship with a primary care-giver is what provides a positive context for early development and learning.	Early interactions impact on the way the brain is 'wired' as well as creating the context for development and learning.
Brain development is linear: in other words, knowledge is gained by a process of accretion throughout life.	Brain development is non-linear: at certain times there are 'sensitive' periods at which conditions for particular kinds of learning are optimal.
Young children's brains are much less active than the brains of adolescents and adults.	In the early years children's brains are much more active than are adults' brains, high levels of activity have reduced considerably by adolescence.

Figure 1.1
Source: From David et al. (2003: 116, adapted from Shore 1997).

Different kinds of societies and their expectations of young children

Studies by anthropologists, psychologists and historians (see, for example, Aries 1962; Bronfenbrenner 1970; Kessen 1979; Morrison [1896] 1995; Cunningham 2006) inform us of the very different childhoods experienced at different times and in different places. Different societies, cultures or subcultures choose different aims for early childhood, whether they spend their time at home with family members or in some form of organized provision. Sometimes the aims are implicit, not openly discussed, decided and shared, and enforced through social pressure on the family and on the child. Sometimes, especially recently in democratic societies, the aims and their consequences are debated, with varying degrees of inclusion and agency among stakeholders.

Rosenthal (2003) analysed the ways in which societies differed in their approaches to the education and care of young children, noting the impact of the cultural context. In societies where individualism and independence are valued, she suggests children are encouraged to learn through play, to be self-reliant and assertive, to show respect for other children as well as for adults and to think independently. Rosenthal's analysis of collectivist societies led her to conclude that here children learn to be interdependent. They identify themselves as responsible members of a social group, cooperate, assume responsibility for others, conform to group norms, are submissive to adult authority and use those traditions and authority as sources of knowledge, memorizing 'known' or 'proven' information. The different valued goals of the two types of society lead in turn to different educational practices. In the individualistic society, children are encouraged to explore, experiment, play and learn through the planning of space, materials, furniture and child-sensitive staff behaviours. Meanwhile, in a collectivist culture, Rosenthal argues, space and materials are organized so that the children can learn through activities planned and structured by the teacher. There are opportunities for rote learning and for imitating the teacher. The children are frequently required to adapt to an adult-led activity, with questioning for which there is a 'correct' answer. Thus a strong sense of belonging is to be instilled in the children, as is respect for the teacher, an authoritarian adult who behaves responsibly and nurtures the children.

Rosenthal cites the United States as an example of the individualist culture and China the collectivist. The study *Preschool in Three Cultures* by Tobin *et al.* (1989), which also includes Japan, provides observational material supporting Rosenthal's analysis, as does a recent film by the celebrated Zhang Huan, *Little Red Flowers*, about a 4-year-old, rebellious boy, Qiang, at his autocratic kindergarten.

Differences can even be seen within a society or culture. Research which demonstrates these differences includes Lubeck's (1986) *Sandbox Society*, about two groups in a US city, and Hartley's (1993) study of three nurseries in the UK. In each study the children are shown to be subject to assumptions by staff that lead to curricula matched to the conditions under which their local communities are living. This is not the same as staff being sensitive to cultural variations and building on that; it is about limiting children's experience and staff expectations of children's potential. For example, in Lubeck's study the children attending a group in a poor black neighbourhood were found to be members of what Rosenthal would call a collectivist culture, learning to be interdependent and to care for and support others. Meanwhile, the children at a group in an affluent white area of the same city were learning to be individualistic, independent and competitive. As Lubeck comments, what is sad is that the children in both those groups were having their development stunted at a time when the world is 'shrinking' and moving out of one's local community or culture is increasingly demanded. There are occasions when each of us needs to be able to give and accept support, as well as those when each of us needs to be brave and assertive.

However, simply instructing early childhood educators to change their practices in order to implement new initiatives aimed at fostering different abilities from those traditionally espoused is no guarantee of success. The process of policy implementation is complex. Vong's (2005) study of the attempt to change the practices of Chinese nursery teachers in order to encourage the growth of entrepreneurs shows how history and tradition impact on and subvert policy makers' intentions, at the same time making aspects of such initiatives their own.

Early literacy

In 1998 members of our Early Years team at Canterbury Christ Church University, funded by the Esmée Fairbairn Foundation, began work on an international project about early print literacy together with colleagues from the University of Melbourne, Australia. We wanted to use documentation, questionnaires, observations and interviews to explore the understandings and practices in early childhood settings in Australia, England, France and Singapore (David *et al.* 2000). A number of important issues and conclusions emerged from our work.

First, we recognized that we would have to abandon hopes of being able to quantify the proportion of time devoted to print literacy learning in any setting or country. The reason for this was that it became obvious that many activities which were not explicitly concerned with print literacy were important experiences contributing to young children's understandings of language and literacy. We were already aware, for example, of the benefits to language and literacy of activities promoting physical development (such as throwing a ball, which helps develop hand–eye coordination), imagination and metacognition. But we began to see that there were occasions when children engaged in play and developed skills and concepts which would ultimately contribute to language, literacy and mathematical proficiency.

By the end of the project we could see the ways in which each society's dominant constructions of early childhood and early childhood education were influencing what the children were expected to do and to achieve. Teachers in Singaporean nurseries felt trapped between the strict demands of parents and primary schools. Although they did not enrol in primary schooling until age 7, the children were required to be capable of writing a 30–40 word story, with correct grammar, in English and, beside other achievements in the English language, they had to speak 600 words and read 400 in Mandarin Chinese. This means that from the age of 2 they were formally instructed in spoken and written English and Mandarin, and taught in English, Chinese, Malay or Tamil. At the same time their government wanted the teachers to give the children greater autonomy and opportunities to learn through play, believing this would develop their entrepreneurial abilities. In contrast, Australian nurseries epitomized Rosenthal's (2003) individualistic culture provision, with no expectation that children would be print literate in any way by the age of admission to primary school. In France, children were immersed in the spoken and written language but again with no expectation before primary school other than love of the French language and their rich cultural heritage. Above all, it seemed, the French nursery experience was about becoming a citizen. Our analysis of the English results demonstrated the confusion and anxiety among practitioners. While roughly half of the 70 questioned believed print literacy should be left until children are 5 or 6 years old, the other half argued that in a print-rich, or print-dependent society children are aware of the power of print from babyhood. The issue then becomes how best to help children learn about print and how it 'works', without destroying a growing love of books, stories and other print media.

Sadly, our observations and discussions in England led us to conclude that the majority of practitioners lacked appropriate training concerning approaches to early literacy, while at the same time believing inspectors would grade them down if they did not demonstrate formal literacy teaching. Children were observed by project team members being called away from deep engagement in play in which relevant, incidental print literacy could have been introduced, to take part in teacher-initiated and teacher-led small group print literacy tasks that were often, clearly, tedious.

Early print literacy

Here in the UK we live in a print-rich, or print-dependent society, so it is important that, as far as is possible, all children become effective readers and writers, people who are both functionally literate and who enjoy engaging with print. At the same time, because they are born sociable, curious and observant, babies and young children are eager to understand and be able to use the power of print. They want to be powerful members of their community and to engage with familiar others in ways they have come to recognize as meaningful. Fifteen-month-old Sebastian points to the print in his favourite picture book, babbling to himself as he does. He has heard the narrative in this text so many times and has seen some of his family members sliding a finger along the print. He knows these marks mean something significant that he loves to hear and, in his own way, repeat. Oliver, when a little older, voluntarily pointed out all the 'Os' in a book he was sharing with a grandparent – not yet 3, he knew 'O' was a significant symbol to him. These were not activities any family member expected or asked for of these very young children but because so much of everyday family life involved the use of print each of the two had made a natural and relaxed start on his literacy journey.

Several years ago, a Danish friend challenged me with the notion that we in the UK put pressure to be print-literate on our young children, even when we do not explicitly undertake to teach in a formal way, even when we think we are providing activities that seem fun. She argued that the children pick this up. I admitted that she could be right and for the ensuing six months returned to this issue daily in my thoughts and sometimes in discussions with colleagues. In the end I came to the conclusion that if we behave as we would in everyday life we are simply exposing the children to the way we live in a print-dependent society and that because these events and activities really are part of life, the children want to be able to take part too. So, the fact that we make notes, read newspapers, letters, bills, adverts, programmes, notices and books, write cards, shopping lists, diaries (one could go on ad infinitum), means we are modelling literate behaviour to the children who share our lives. Given appropriate materials, or props, young children will use them and show they know a lot about literate behaviour – as long as they have observed adults and older children engaging in them. What they actually write will be meaningful to them.

While playing at cafés with her mother and grandmother, 2-year-old Coralie was asked for a menu. She could have used a book but her grandmother gave her a piece of folded paper. She immediately took it to a nearby table, asked for a pen and wrote a copious menu, which was then studied by the 'customers'.

In David *et al.* (2000), we argued, on the basis of others' and our own research, that in general children in this age group need to be offered opportunities to learn about the 'big picture' of print literacy, not the fine detail, which is probably meaningless until one has a grasp of the big picture and until one can understand that although a cup is a cup whichever way up it is, a letter 'b', for example, is not. Further, 'big picture' knowledge is gained more through experience than through formal instruction, the latter being an inappropriate approach to teaching very young children.

Coralie's menu

What we have to ask ourselves is why the rush to have children experience formal literacy instruction so early? Do we believe that the earlier they begin formal literacy instruction the more proficient they will be and in greater numbers? The trouble is, this seems to me rather like expecting that if you hurtle along a motorway in your car, children will gain knowledge of the places they are passing if a parent tells them about the places. Comprehension without meaningful experience is difficult even for adults. Most of our European partner countries leave the start of literacy until children begin primary school at either age 6 or 7 and their later results are better, with fewer teenagers and adults functionally illiterate. Some argue that the quirky nature of the English language requires an early start. Yet, strangely, the phonics system that is advocated for that early, formally taught start cannot assist with words like bough, tough, thought, and so on.

Messages for parents such as advising them to have magnetic fridge door letters for play with their young children, because they have been linked to reading success, seem like a quick fix unless parents are also helped to understand that this is only a small part of a panoply of family behaviours involving using and enjoying print. It is also important to help parents see that all sorts of play activities foster their children's learning and development in different areas and that limiting their involvement with their children to adult-dominated literacy activities may result in stunting development in other areas. It may also make children disenchanted with reading and writing, rather than eager to use this powerful means of communication and source of enjoyment.

Research (see, for example, Hannon et al. 1991; Hannon 2000; Raban and Nolan 2005) demonstrates that parents are eager to help their children acquire literacy skills and are capable of doing so irrespective of their socio-economic background, but they do not always possess the range of information they feel they need to promote that learning appropriately. As Raban and Nolan (2005: 296) suggest:

> Parents need relevant information about ways to enhance literacy experiences at home and this information needs to be culturally sensitive and easily accessible, as literacy still stands as one of the best chances for individual upward mobility.

Simply telling parents to get a set of magnetic letters and to share story books with their young children is not enough.

What are the most important 'tasks' of early childhood?

Each phase of life could be seen as a time to face new challenges, new tasks. Can we decide what the tasks of these earliest years might be? And who decides what they might be?

Clearly, most babies set themselves many tasks, such as being accepted and appreciated as a member of their family, making sense and meaning of what they observe, being able to communicate, being mobile, finding out about the world and people around them, and becoming more independent. This range of complex tasks, which most children appear to achieve with speed and relative ease, requires holistic development, rather than development that can be separated into 'boxes' labelled cognitive, emotional, and so on. All aspects of development interweave and, similarly, meaning making depends on understanding many different forms of communication. As Marsh (2004: 52) points out, there has now been extensive research indicating a need for wider definitions of literacy 'which incorporate technology and multi-modal ways of making meaning'.

While young children have probably always been expert observers who are highly literate in interpreting body language (David *et al.* 2003), the expansion of media and technology in recent years, and the likelihood that there is much more to come, should alert us to their need to engage with these forms too. Certainly we know from the adeptness and confidence with which children use computers and related electronic equipment that these are aspects of their lives in which they are deeply interested.

However, these 'other literacies' should not be taken for granted. 'People literacy' – the ability to 'read' other people emotionally and socially and respond appropriately – is an essential aspect of living in a civilized, democratic society. Goleman (1996, 2006) has pointed out how emotional and social intelligence can be fostered, as well as showing the consequences of leaving these to chance, 'road rage' being but one example.

What makes sense to young children?

So, if young children are setting themselves tasks – often the same tasks that are set implicitly by their families and carers – what is the adult's role in helping them to achieve all this and to make sense of their lives? Most importantly, adults need to observe and decode what babies and young children are trying to do. In the case of communication this will be through looks and gestures, then increasingly through utterances and eventually through drawing and writing. So adults need to make language learning meaningful and often fun, combining it with sensory experiences and in step with the child's pace (Tassoni 2006).

What will not make sense to young children, in fact what may even prove stressful for them, is:

- having to sit still for long periods of time;
- being unable to be very active;
- not being able to make decisions for themselves;
- having to be involved in a task which does not interest or motivate them;
- being unable to succeed at tasks;
- finding it difficult to concentrate;
- not being able to understand or relate concepts to their own experiences.

(Scott and Stevens 2006: 136)

Phonics teaching will only make sense once children have played with sounds and come to understand smaller and smaller units of sound in different stages of phonological awareness. As Scott and Stevens (2006) point out, these stages are: the development of auditory awareness (being able to discriminate general sounds and speech sounds); having an awareness of rhythm and beat (so they can recognize syllables); rhyming skills (awareness of onset and rime); and phonemic awareness (being able to register alliteration and recognize individual phonemes).

Wasting young children's time

As Tassoni (2006) points out, tuning in to the sounds of the English language is a prerequisite for understanding phonics. She adds that this can make life difficult for children who have not been exposed to spoken English in their earliest years. (Perhaps one should also be alert to regional pronunciation; for example, my Liverpudlian husband jokingly mocks my 'Manchester' pronunciation of hair, while himself declaring the word to be pronounced like 'fur'.)

Further, there has been much hand-wringing of late about the extent to which boys are disaffected about reading and especially about writing. In the early years (and maybe throughout life!), boys are generally more mobile than girls, spending more time in activities in which they can move around and disliking activities which confine their movements. In part this may be attributable to the (generally) relatively immature central nervous system of males at birth, which in turn leads to different handling by parents and carers. Clearly social conditioning may be a major contributing factor, as boys observe older males being more demonstrably active than females and since they are still frequently encouraged to be so. Making children, whether girls or boys, sit down and trying to engage them in teacher-led activities for which they have no foundational knowledge and which do not inspire them is simply wasting their precious time.

Their time is being wasted if they are being asked to take part in activities which are meaningless to them and for which they also have no foundational knowledge.

What is early childhood for?

The question of what early childhood is 'for' is said to have been the focus of debate by parents, practitioners and policy makers in their plaza debates in Reggio Emilia, Italy (Edwards *et al.* 1998) as they developed their world-renowned nursery provision and today, as they continually re-evaluate their work. Most societies have no such debates, assuming that there is an obvious answer to what any phase of life is 'for'. As society changes, there is always a more urgent need to examine the status quo against new ideas. Just over a hundred years ago, it was thought essential to have a workforce for our industrial society (David 2006) that was basically literate and numerate, but also one that was biddable. The school curriculum was therefore elementary and taught very didactically by a transmission method. Now, however, we live in a post-industrial, information society and our needs to live in and contribute to that society are very different from those required a century, or even 20 years ago. Change and the expansion of knowledge and information is too rapid for a human being to be able to keep pace, so we need to educate children to know how and where to access any information they need. Of course, they also need to be literate and numerate to read and process that information but they need other skills and knowledge too. They also need positive attitudes to the process of learning, to be zestful, curious and creative about the exploration, experimentation, discovery, interpretation, representation and transformation of knowledge about their world.

Unfortunately childhood, especially early childhood, is seen as a preparation for and subsidiary to adulthood. After over 40 years as a practitioner, researcher and, most importantly, observer of young children, my own conclusion is that early childhood is important in its own right, a phase in life when the tasks we set ourselves and are set by others may indeed be foundations for later, but they are intrinsically valuable. It is a time when we are intent on comprehending life, love and death – how we live together, loving and being loved/ lovable, the world around us, and all that is in it, and how things work. We gain that understanding through observing the people, creatures, objects and places that are familiar and interacting with them in ways that make sense to us.

Note

[1] The choice of age 5 in the UK was the result of pressure on Parliament from industrialists and not through any consideration of children's development.

References

Aries, P. (1962) *Centuries of Childhood*. London: Jonathan Cape.

Bronfenbrenner, U. (1970) *The Two Worlds of Childhood: US and USSR*. New York: Russell Sage Foundation.

Cunningham, H. (2006) *The Invention of Childhood*. London: BBC Worldwide.

David, T. (2006) The world picture, in G. Pugh and B. Duffy (eds) *Contemporary Issues in the Early Years*, 4th edition. London: Sage Publications.

David, T., Raban, B., Ure, C., Goouch, K., Jago, M., Barrière, I. and Lambirth, A. (2000) *Making Sense of Early Literacy: A Practitioner's Perspective*. Stoke-on-Trent: Trentham Books.

David, T., Goouch, K., Powell, S. and Abbott, L. (2003) *Birth to Three Matters: A Review of the Literature*, Research Report 444. London: DfES.

Edwards, C., Gandini, L. and Foreman, G. (eds) (1998) *The Hundred Languages of Children: The Reggio Emilia Approach to Early Childhood Education*. Norwood, NJ: Ablex.

Goleman, D. (1996) *Emotional Intelligence*. London: Bloomsbury.

Goleman, D. (2006) *Social Intelligence*. London: Hutchinson.

Hannon, P. (2000) *Reflecting on Literacy in Education*. London: Routledge Falmer.

Hannon, P., Weinberger, J. and Nutbrown, C. (1991) A study of work with parents to promote early literacy development, *Research Papers in Education*, 6(2): 77–97.

Hartley, D. (1993) *Understanding Nursery Education: A Sociological Analysis*. London: Cassell.

Kessen, W. (1979) The American child and other cultural inventions, *American Psychologist*, 34(10): 815–20.

Lubeck, S. (1986) *Sandbox Society*. Lewes: Falmer Press.

Marsh, J. (2004) The techno-literacy practices of young children, *Journal of Early Childhood Research*, 2(1): 51–66.

Morrison, A. ([1896] 1995) *A Child of the Jago*. Chicago, IL: Academy Chicago Publishers.

Raban, B. and Nolan, A. (2005) Reading practices experienced by preschool children in areas of disadvantage, *Journal of Early Childhood Research*, 3(3): 289–98.

Rosenthal, M. (2003) Quality in early childhood education and care: a cultural context, *European Early Childhood Education Research Journal*, 11(2): 101–16.

Scott, K. and Stevens, J. (2006) Stages, not ages, in S. Featherstone, (ed.) *L is for Sheep: Getting Ready for Phonics*. Lutterworth: Featherstone Education.

Shore, R. (1997) *Rethinking the Brain*. New York: Families and Work Institute.

Tassoni, P. (2006) Tuning in, in S. Featherstone, (ed.) *L is for Sheep: Getting Ready for Phonics*. Lutterworth: Featherstone Education.

Tobin, J., Wu, D. and Davidson, D. (1989) *Preschool in Three Cultures*. New Haven, CT: Yale University Press.

Vong, K.I. (2005) Towards a creative early childhood programme in Zhuhai-SER and Macau-SER of the People's Republic of China. Unpublished doctoral thesis, University of London.

2 Parents' voices: a conversation with parents of pre-school children

Kathy Goouch

The idea that children's first reading lessons occur at home, within families and communities, is not a new idea. The work of Spufford, Vincent and other social historians and children's literature specialists, in a wonderfully understated text *Opening the Nursery Door* (Hilton *et al.* 1997), provides evidence that, from as early as the seventeenth century, very young children were being taught to read at home, often with home-made materials, religious tracts and broadsheets and through fairy stories, moral tales and 'pleasurable texts' (Hilton *et al.* 1997: 3). Such home literacy lessons were not confined to the wealthy; there seems to be clear evidence throughout history that children from poor families were also able to read from an early age, taught by their mothers or other women in the community. In Minns's report of Irish born children living in the English Midlands in the mid-nineteenth century, she tells of one son's description of his mother:

> She never learned to write, but she could read and she taught her own children, reading Irish sermons aloud to them. She also told them the stories of Oisen, Fin, and Cuchullan, and the Gobawn Sayre, as well as singing and reciting 'a goodly number of old Irish songs and poems'. This was the same women who spent hours sorting dusty rags and rotting bones on the brick floor of their two-roomed house, transferring a life of rural poverty to one of urban survival. And yet Mrs Barclay probably taught her own children to read by doing intuitively what good reading teachers ... have always done – by sharing her deep enthusiasm and using a range of strategies and texts to support her children's reading development.
>
> (Minns 1997: 181)

In an examination of the curriculum in the nineteenth century, the relationship between the 'domestic curriculum' and the 'official curriculum' is explored, with children before and outside of formal school learning 'by imitation, experiment and casual instruction from everyone they met... the task of gaining command over the tools of written communication was merely one amongst many, and it was far from being the most difficult' (Vincent 1997: 169). From the work of social historians it seems that poverty was not itself a barrier to learning to read, although the acquisition of literacy skills themselves was not necessarily understood as a priority, a skill of worth or a key to a better life. School, and the introduction of certain religious or moral texts to children, was seen by the authorities of the time to be the way to improve children's minds rather than their position in life or for broader economic and employment purposes. These texts, however, appeared to be a disincentive for school attendance, which was not yet compulsory. During this period of history, Vincent describes how 'inspected schools' had to rethink their decision not to allow 'literary anthologies' into schools in an effort to encourage children's attendance, as these texts had been felt to distract and over-stimulate. Interesting too that, by the middle of the nineteenth century, it had been noted that 'the fragments of words and sentences which it (the child) faced in the classroom bore no visible relation to the complex linguistic skills which had been mastered in infancy and early childhood' (Vincent: 166). Before 1852, Vincent describes how 'it had never been very clear how the child was to connect the syllables and word lists either to its oral vocabulary or to the tasks of reading and writing joined up paragraphs' and how, at school, the 'inevitable strangeness of print had become unnecessarily absolute' (166). And so the curriculum was revised to ensure that 'lessons should consist entirely of words with which the ear of children is familiar' and that children's lessons should 'contain matters which shall be interesting to him' (Vincent: 167). In this way, connections could be made between what the child had learned at home and new learning occurring in school. More recent research has also demonstrated the value of this kind of contextual learning, at home, at the point of interest and with texts that matter to the child, and by intuitive parents and carers (Brice Heath 1983; Wells 1986; Wood 1988; Rogoff 1990).

If these debates sound familiar, it is because, more than a century and a half later, academics, policy makers and politicians are still troubling about exactly these same issues: what, if anything, are children learning at home about reading? Is it possible to extend this in school contexts? Should learning to read be a 'pleasurable' activity and, importantly, should the teaching of reading be 'particularistic' or holistic in relation to school texts?

In exploring the social context of learning and reading lessons more than a hundred and fifty years ago, Vincent and other social historians have been anxious to discover what parents thought themselves about the curriculum on offer to their children during this period of history. Tracing and tracking such information, that is views and opinions from past centuries, is a difficult if not an impossible task now. Even today, the relationship between home and school, between home literacy and school literacy, is still often only reported from official sources. In this twenty-first century, while plenty in the media and in politics claim to represent parents' views, the opinions of parents and carers are rarely directly sought or directly cited.

For the purpose of this chapter, a small group of parents of pre-school children were gathered together simply to hear their understandings of early reading 'lessons', the 'domestic curriculum' of Vincent's social research, and of their views and visions of their children's first steps into school. There was no attempt to make this a representative sample, in any usual sense, and in fact, by their own definition, this group claim to be all from the middle class. There are five families represented by seven parents and they have between them eleven children. The group are casual acquaintances who have met locally through their children's nursery or swimming clubs, dance classes or at the park. The group were gathered informally in the company of two researchers and their responses were recorded. While their conversation ranged at times across the subject of literacy learning, specific questions were asked as prompts at various times to focus the responses and these have been gathered here under three headings: *Literacy activities at home, Expectations of school* and *Progression*. Transcription of the parents' own words are drawn together to offer fragments of the picture of how some children journey from the early stages towards their parents' expectations of literacy competence.

Literacy activities at home

If you would just help us by telling us about the ways you engage your children in literacy at home and the sorts of things you do to encourage your child to become a reader.

Liz:	When I can hear him waking up about 6ish I go in and put a whole pile of books in his cot and he sits there for about an hour reading them. It's fantastic!
Louise:	We have been reading to Dan and Bella since they were about six weeks. It was from when I first started

to have them on my own when I thought, 'Ok, what am I going to do now!'

Lisa: Bedtime stories are a must every night but also he likes books because we have read to him since he was about six months so now going to bed he is trying to extend his bedtime so we have decided that if he sits in his room with a big pile of books it is fine which he 'reads' himself. We take the pile of books away at night and then we tell him that mummy will sneak in when he is asleep and when he wakes up he has also got his pile of books. And again we don't know for how long but his wake up time is later and later and he is there reading his books.

Marianna: She also has audio stories which I leave on at night so that she goes to sleep, again she can never get enough, always wants another story.

Julie: He has his books on the bookshelf that he can reach in his bedroom so he can go and help himself. He also likes comics, which he chooses from Waitrose every time we go in, normally chosen because of the toy on the front rather than the stories themselves. But he works through those and likes the activities in there and wants us to read what to do. He also likes to do computer games, CBeebies; he has started to recognize words such as the start button; he recognizes the shape of it.

Andrew: Accessibility, making sure there are books and things always around. But also associating writing with drawing; he has been doing letters from quite early on. CH for Charlie – that's an association with drawing which is definitely fun and not distinguishing from drawing and making letters just as he does drawing pictures.

Julie: He likes to leave signs around. I don't know if you had noticed on the front door 'Charlie's tea party'. He made me write it down on a piece of paper so he could copy and stick it on the door. In the lounge room there is 'the football room', so he is really getting into the whole message thing, telling people things by writing down. The other thing which I mentioned before is that he likes to read; have read to him the titles of TV programmes, eg Fifi and the Flowerpots all have opening titles.

Andrew: He does do the crossword on the back of the *Evening Standard* if we bring it home; he squiggles in each of the boxes.

Louise: If I'm doing the shopping lists they will both fetch a little pad and write the shopping list with me.

These groups of children are presented, as babies and toddlers, with the idea that books and stories have high status in their families. The parents are also keen to extend children's experiences beyond printed texts towards audio and forms of popular culture including comics, television and computer software. Quite naturally, the responses included references to writing and mark-making activities as this parent group confidently made connections between literacy modes, with their children learning valuable early lessons about print functions and print conventions.

Inevitably, the conversation turned to the parents' own literary beginnings:

Lisa: As an only child reading was my absolute salvation. I didn't have books just to play with; my mum worked a lot, so reading was my escape. I don't think I would be where I am now if I hadn't loved reading and found it as my escape; and knowing the ladies down the library, having a relationship with them, who used to encourage me to take out books, and say have you looked at this or whatever. That was very important.

Out of all the things you described, what do you think is the most important thing for you?

All: Reading with them.

Lisa: Making them love reading in whatever that is, whether it's listening to cassettes along with a picture book or reading. Making them enjoy it without being stressful or difficult, making it fun and them enjoying it and then certainly my little boy is much younger than everyone else's. For him at the moment it's about making him realize that I am reading so if he has got his hands over the words because he wants to pore over the pictures and then says 'Why have you stopped, Mummy?' it's making that connection, while I'm running my finger under the words as I'm saying them so he realizes. We are just starting to get a bit of curiosity and I think what we were saying is so important to them, that idea about their own name. It's a great starting point to getting them to draw letters and getting them to recognize T for Toby or CH for Charlie; it makes them feel important knowing their name in a written form.

Andrew: I suspect that perhaps I couldn't pinpoint one most important thing but it's actually the blend and the access to reading and writing in which ever form it's in as different people learn in different ways and at different times. If software is the thing of the week with Charlie then we will just go full on with that, but if it's bedtime stories or Dora the Explorer on TV, it's being open to literacy in every form.

One very important focus with the parents' responses seems to be the closeness of adults to children in home literacy events and the parents' sensitivity and awareness of their children's interests and development. They appeared to be happy to support their children by following their lead. This led us to ask for more specific information about styles of interaction. Evidently 'talk' is central, with repetition, rhyming, response to stories and illustrations, as well as oral tales all becoming key elements of reported home literacy.

When you are reading to your child what sort of things go on between you?

Liz: We talk a lot about pictures because I think for them it's actually the pictures that are more important when you are reading to them. They aren't really interested particularly in the words; they are looking at the picture. So we talk a lot about the picture and the characters.

Lisa: We use a lot of rhyming books. Toby just loves them and after reading them about four times I will read a line and he will tell me the next line. He's not reading it but he will tell me!

Marianna: They have a memory like a sponge. I think it's generally the same – we have a conversation around the story: why is he unhappy; what do you think; why do you think he did that?

Andrew: Charlie occasionally asks for a story, not a book. He asks for us to make a story up, just sit and make a story. We have a series of flying horse stories that we have made up about a flying horse that comes and takes him somewhere. He occasionally makes up a story of his own, his own little fantasy world.

Louise: It's special for him; he feels quite special.

Liz: You have to let them lead.

Louise: Otherwise it becomes a chore; they need to have that love of reading.

It is clear that books and stories are central to these children's lives; their parents consider them to be important. While story tapes and computer software are also mentioned, constant access to books and stories, and to parents as readers and storytellers, are the key focus of these parents' literacy engagements with their children. Equally significant in this set of responses is the strength of feeling about the importance of developing in children a keen enjoyment and love of books. This group of children is supported by parents who are following their lead in self-motivated reading events. While 'fun' and a love of reading appears to be the motivating factor, the parents also identified learning opportunities for their children, for example repetition and the use of rhyming texts, the need for children to scrutinize illustrations and the identification of print as part of the storytelling process. Another key aspect of these early learning experiences is the emphasis on response to stories and books. The parents are not simply reading the stories but also developing conversations with their children around them, asking and answering questions, talking about characters and modelling response to literature. Important, too, is the developing interconnectedness of reading, writing and talk. While there seemed to be clear consensus about the value of these early reading activities at home, starting school was looming for most of the families.

Expectations of school

What do you think is going to happen in terms of teaching and reading when your children start school? What are you expecting?

Julie: Well, I'm hoping that the enjoyment carries on then, that Charlie goes into a classroom where reading is just a part of things. I saw his new classroom yesterday, because he is starting in September, and there is a reading area there and I am hoping that he will be able to just wander over and be able to pick up a book he likes and read the books. I am slightly worried that that might not be the case; I am slightly worried that his access to books will be restricted and that reading might become a chore rather than a fun thing that it is now. But you know I'm hopeful that, because he hasn't started yet, that he will have a teacher that makes reading fun. So you know he will carry on through to his secondary school enjoying reading.

Andrew: I'm really hoping that reading for its own sake will continue, will continue to be fun. But reading will be a vehicle for other things; intuitively when you talk about reading and literacy you think of stories. My childhood memories are of reading encyclopaedias.

Marianna: My worry is that of a class of 30 children you can't rely on the teacher to press them forward; that the onus is still with you to encourage them.

Liz: And teaching styles as well: if the teacher has a class of 30 children how can you tailor that to individual reading? How are they going to learn to read most effectively themselves?

Julie: For me it's the fact that he just likes reading. That's the most important thing.

Marianna: I just get the feeling that some of these schemes, or whatever, are just gearing them up to pass these exams, these SATs and things that they have to do. We all like reading different things, and I don't know how much choice they get in what books they read. Whether they have to tick the list that they have read this one and this one, in order to get to the end of Reception Year target and then Year 1 and Year 2.

Liz: I think it's combining the two, though. I think it's doing the kind of structured stuff and at the same time allowing them to go to the library and pick a book and allowing them to read a book that they can read easily so that they can enjoy it. Its combining the two; I do think you need the structure. I think the children like the structure, they like the routine, they like to know where they are – it gives them more control.

Marianna: Not being at school yet I don't really know how much flexibility there is, and what books they really know.

> If there was a particular book, say that he is not interested in, they wouldn't send him home and say he has got to read it?
>
> *Matt:*   I expect that Janet, John or the equivalent will build a more formal side, a more structured side. Because I'm no expert, so trying to take them forward in what they are doing is more difficult. If you have a series of books like I read when I was a little lad ... Another issue: I remember being obsessed with one book, I can't remember what it was, and I wanted to read, and I read it about ten times, and I don't think that developed my reading, and I don't know when that was, age 5 or 6 or something. That wasn't developing my reading – if the teacher is controlling 30 kids, putting an individually tailored scheme that is leading somewhere together is going to be tough.

It is interesting to note in this section the tension that appears to exist in the parents' minds. They are firm in their belief that their children's experience of reading should continue to be rich and enjoyable. There also appears to be an almost innate faith in the school as an institution and in teachers as professionals. And so, while there are worries about structure and inflexibility and class sizes being expressed, there is also an underlying trust in structure for development. Whether or not their children enjoy reading is still the central theme here, although acknowledgement of systems, schemes and structures is also in evidence. Only one response considers the possibility that there may be a partnership involved in supporting the children: 'The onus is still with you to encourage them.' Class size quite naturally worries them.

The focus was then deliberately moved towards the teaching of phonics.

Are you aware of the current moves to teach children to read by synthetic phonics 'first, fast and only'?

The parents seemed to be completely unaware of the consequences of the new developments in forefronting phonics and focusing singly on synthetic phonics, following the Rose Review (Rose 2006). The researchers were urged to provide information and gave a brief factual overview, describing the nature of 'synthetic phonics' and 'the simple view of reading'. The parents were then extremely vocal in their responses.

Andrew: It would be a real shame if individual teachers weren't allowed to innovate and that type of thing.

Liz: Will it be made fun?

Andrew: I would be saddened to think that we were saddling kids with the one size fits all; this is the way thou shall learn to read. I compare it a bit with the way French kids are taught to write; all French writing is the same. So I have a sense that the debate over phonics is a bit headline grabbing.

Marianna: Sounds like a big marketing thing to me.

Julie: Is this driven by corporates or is it driven by academics?

Andrew: Or corporates with pseudo-academic credentials.

Marianna: If somebody is doing well in their phonics and they show a capability for literacy, what are they going to do if they have to read Shakespeare? It's a good building block but I don't think it should be the only thing.

Lisa: I'm sure it's really effective, and I think they are probably right but what it ignores is the bond, the love of reading and that sort of thing is what reading with your children and encouraging them to read is all about.

Matt: But I don't think we are very representative around this table, and lots of kids will be getting to school, their brain has been developed beyond what their input has been so far. So if you want to leap frog up the kids who have never ever been in front of a book before then maybe there is some science that says this is the best way of doing it and I would want to say that my gut feeling from my background says that phonics is a bit suspect, but it may just be that in certain cases it's the best way of doing things.

Marianna: It goes back to the achieving the attainment goals that they have got; you can get them there fast but do they enjoy it?

Liz: There is no point learning how to read if you don't want to use it.

Julie: Won't it let those children that don't like to learn in that kind of way fall by the wayside, so you have high achievers, like Joshua, who love that kind of learning, but then you have kids that recognize shapes. Like I said earlier that Charlie recognizes the shape of the start button on the computer game. I thought that was brilliant when he first started doing that, so kids who learn by recognizing shapes are not going to be recognized in their achievements, because they are not doing the sounds.

Andrew: We have also got to remember that sitting here is also a bunch of rather middle-class parents, who have talked about a variety of methods we have used beforehand. What about the kids who haven't had that exposure to literacy before school? If they have had no exposure pre-school and then they have Jolly Phonics, I fear for those kids.

Julie: It's about being fun before school. If they get into school and the only literacy they have seen is signs and, you know, the things that they can't avoid then they haven't had the fun experience of sitting down with their mums and dads and enjoying the pictures and the stories etc. So they get to school and the first thing they sit and do is recite some sounds, and that's not fun.

Liz: Joshua will automatically look at the picture to guess the word; I can see him doing it. You can't give him a book with no pictures because then it's not enjoyable.

Julie: It's also disrespectful to the kids because it's assuming that they don't have the intelligence to work through the learning styles that are offered to them.

Liz: It's suppressing their natural instincts to guess and work it out.

Julie: We know as adult readers when you are reading avidly you never finish the line, do you, so you are guessing the last bit anyway. So it's going to be restricting their adult reading, because they will be poring over the words.

Lisa: It doesn't seem to teach fluency; it's very focused on word rather than sentence.

Louise: It's not looking at the whole picture is it?

Liz: I don't see why it has to be unique; I don't see why you can't use a combination of different things?

Louise: Just that it being so structured and looking at that only you are denying the children that richness of reading. You talked about the bond, and just the experience of being a child. It seems to me just one more step to reduce the experience and the freedom of childhood, which to gain their growth skills and general communication skills before we then start to do, what I guess you would term broadly educational stuff, teaching them to recognise sounds and words. I strongly feel that if they don't have that richness of experience then it is a great loss.

Matt: Well you can balance that; if that's the way it's being done you can balance it out.

Lisa: Only if you are a middle-class parent, who has got time to do it.

The parents in this group are all graduates, professionals in their own lives and completely informed about the development of their babies and toddlers in terms of health and welfare from birth through their children's pre-school years. However, they professed to know little about new reforms in the teaching of reading that would directly affect their children on entry into school. Again there was a sense of innate trust that the schools they had chosen would 'get it right'. At the suggestion that there would be a 'one size fits all' approach with synthetic phonics as the 'first, fast and only' way that children would be taught to read in the early years of school, this group of parents expressed concern, not just that the diverse learning needs of their own children might not be met in this way, but also for other children who they felt may not have had the advantage of rich pre-school literacy experiences at home, which they saw as being a positive introduction to the benefits of learning to read. One parent tried a comparison with the way he felt that children learned numeracy skills:

Andrew: I think the same applies to numeracy, the way kids learn to count. It's a variety of stimuli and methods and you could argue that if there is any form, any area of learning that lends itself to something more rigorous and analytical as this phonics approach sounds you could apply that to numeracy, but I can't.

Although critical appraisal of the impact of education policy had not before occurred to them, the parents were quick to begin to analyse how children learn in all areas and to try to understand the influences and impulses driving policy for their children's schooling. It is interesting to note that at one point they began a cynical response to the 'corporate' or economic gains to be made! The parents also made connections with adult literacy and how undue attention to each word limited fluency. One parent's comment, 'You can get them there fast but do they enjoy it?' is particularly apposite in today's political climate when attainment in reading appears to be a greater goal than engagement in reading events. Also, there was a clear assumption by one parent, based on her own experience, that children 'naturally' want to 'guess and work it out', that reading may be a problem-solving activity.

Throughout the session, the parents seemed to be confident that their children's interest and engagement in reading events was central to learning to read.

> *Julie:* When you go into my son's nursery school, you go in there during the day and you catch them at reading time, the kids are just rapt; they are sitting there, they are still, there is no noise. You think they would be doing it all day because the kids absolutely love it.

A 'challenge' was offered by the researchers to this vignette:

That's all very nice but they need to be learning their skills . . .

> *Liz:* But they are learning skills.
> *Marianna:* They are learning to listen, they are learning to communicate in non-verbal ways.
> *Louise:* They are using their imagination.

The parents were very quickly able to offer a very confident set of passionately expressed responses to the idea that skills in reading could be narrowed to exclude the wide range of abilities they felt essential to the process.

Progression

Do you think they are getting on quite well (in reading)?

At this end stage of the conversation, the parents were really beginning to express their uncertainty about the system in schools. They began to wonder about two very important issues. First, they were starting to question exactly what was being measured. They acknowledged the importance of significant growth or learning points in children's development – clearly this mirrors parents' awe and excitement at every aspect of their children's growth and development. But, importantly, as they had emphasized throughout that love of stories and books was an important factor, they expressed concern that this might be ignored now:

> *Andrew:*   It's harder to measure love of literacy or love of reading. The intuitive feeling is to break down the milestones, for the breakthroughs. The first time he does something, wow, whether it's the first time he writes his name or the first time he picks out a word, you see him coming up another level.
>
> *Julie:*   For me it's the fact that he just likes reading.

Secondly, another significant concern for the parents here is that if only phonic knowledge is being taught and therefore only phonic knowledge is learned by the children, then where do the children go if that fails them? One parent was able to offer a comparison between two systems that her children had encountered:

> *Louise:*   I was going to say that mine used to go to a day nursery that was very structured and they do a lot of writing and were getting to the point where they could write their names when we moved here. The nursery they go to now is very play-based and they do very little sitting down, very little pencil control and they have lost that. I'm not too worried as they still maintain the enjoyment of what they are doing rather than it being a chore and at 4 for heaven's sake, if you lose them here you have lost it. So I want them to maintain the passion.

'How will they teach children to read 'sausage'?'

There was a clear consensus amongst the parents that their children should enjoy books and stories and that by enjoying literacy events they would learn to read and to read well. Sensibly, the parents were also aware that their children were most interested currently in decoding words that mattered to them, like 'sausage' and 'dinosaur', so they challenged the idea of instructing children in sounds and phonically regular words, without supporting contexts.

Unlike the children in Vincent's research, the children of the parents in this discussion group will not absent themselves from school if they are not motivated or inspired by the content of their texts or their day.

Children today generally tend to be compliant at school and to seek to please the adults caring for them, although there is still the danger that some may become disaffected, disinterested in the range of texts, or the requirements and activities around texts, or in their perceptions of their own abilities in reading. Attendance and compliance, however, are not enough to ensure achievement, personal fulfilment or to nourish and sustain a love of literacy and literature. Like Mrs Barclay in Minns's research (cited above), and like this group of parents, teachers need to demonstrate their own enthusiasm, as well as using a range of strategies, to motivate young children towards engagement in literacy. To achieve this, however, clear acknowledgement needs to be made that engagement, enthusiasm and enjoyment, obviously key elements in this group of children's early reading experiences, are all central to achievement in learning to read at school.

While officers responsible to central governments are incessantly busy compiling new instructions and prescriptions for the teaching of reading, they may be interested in the idea that the content of the curriculum should perhaps contain material 'with which the ear of children is familiar'. In the case of the children from the families in this research, that would be the rich collection of tuneful texts including at least picture fiction, story tapes, CBeebies stories, comics, computer stories, menus, recipes and stories told by family storytellers. Anything less would be disrespectful to the early literacy experiences carefully sculpted in families. The parents in this study, as most do, used their own reading histories to inform their parenting and literacy decisions:

> I remember when I was a kid, I loved reading. I remember that my younger sister didn't and so I like to see that Charlie will actively go to his bookshelf and sit there and choose a book or will ask for stories through the day. Whether he is sitting on the toilet or ... you know. Sometimes it is a strain for us, but he loves it.

In this child's literacy-rich world, books are literally everywhere. It will be interesting to see if his new school can sustain not only the range of texts but also the range of spaces and places to read!

This group of parents had watched their children develop literacy competence and affective engagement in literacy events up to the start of school at 4, with very little, if any, reference to letters sounds. They appeared hardly to have thought beyond the fact that they had helped their children's love of literacy and that they hoped it would continue. Having chosen their children's first school, based on a range of personal issues or geographic location, they now appeared to trust the system. The suggestion that children's uniqueness may not be considered in a 'one size fits all' approach appeared shocking to them. These parents, close observers of their children's development and progress, were easily able to understand some of the subtle implications of the implementation of the Independent Review of the Teaching of Early Reading (2006) and the impact that it may have. Far from depending on central government to deliver 'a simple view of reading', they seemed to expect a curriculum based on a professional approach to teaching young children to read, hoping that schools would help their children to 'maintain the passion'. It will be of great interest, after these 11 children have started their first year at school, to discover if they have retained their interest in books and stories, to learn how they learned to read 'sausage' and whether or not their parents still put enjoyment and love of reading at the top of their wish list.

Finally ...

Brice Heath's seminal work on language, literacy, communities and culture (Brice Heath 1983) has influenced a generation of students and teachers and, from her studies, comparisons can be made between this group of parents and the 'townspeople', whose children bring with them to school:

> linguistic and cultural capital accumulated through hundreds of thousands of occasions for practising the skills and espousing the values the schools transmit ... Their socially determined habits and values have created for them an ideology in which all that they do makes sense to their current identity and their preparations for the achievements which will frame their future.
>
> (Brice Heath 1983: 368)

If it is true, as the transcripts above suggest, that even this group of parents, most closely associated with school, express concern at the narrowing of teaching approaches and subject content in relation to the teaching of reading, then it is difficult to understand from where or for whose purposes the mandate for synthetic phonics first, fast and only has been commissioned. To counteract government arguments about their concerns for the 15 per cent of so called 'underachievers', the processes of socialization and acculturation need also to be considered. It seems that social, economic and political structures:

impel parents or other members of the family to interact with children in different ways, assign different tasks and reward and punish different ways of behaving ... in accordance with the demands which the environments place on individuals and groups.

(Mishra *et al.* 1996: 89)

Acculturation has been explained by the same authors as an imbalanced 'flow of cultural elements' to enable a dominant cultural group to 'change the economic, linguistic, religious and other cultural features of the local, subordinate group towards its own standards' (Mishra *et al.* 1996: 112). It could be argued, then, that in its haste to 'acculturate' all children through school systems, governments may be missing the reality of the social contexts into which children are growing and developing. If, as Brice Heath claims, some governments force teachers to 'transmit only mainstream language and culture patterns' then inevitably there will be children in the early stages who fail because they fail to make connections between their own early learned language(s) and mainstream language.

In the task- and target-driven education system that currently prevails it is hard to see how the 'passion' for reading described by the parents in this chapter can be sustained. We learned from their parents that 'Josh is interested in finding out what things say', that 'Charlie likes to know what the titles of TV programmes say' , that 'Toby loves rhyming books' and 'Selena likes picture dictionaries', and that Andrew makes up flying horses stories for his son. Other children from other families will have had different experiences with different texts, some mediated by parents and others perhaps not. There will be, however, some commonly held assumptions amongst all children entering school for the first time. They will probably all be expecting to be able to make text choices, they will be joyful at finding familiar texts, books or stories, they will want to share their enjoyment of books and stories, to be able to laugh at them, be puzzled by them and to be helped to understand them, by their friends and by their teachers. It seems strange and rather cruel that some children, whatever shape their first culturally defined literacy experiences may have taken, will not have such positive early reading lessons in school.

References

Brice Heath, S. (1983) *Ways with Words*. Cambridge: Cambridge University Press.

Hilton, M., Styles, M. and Watson, V. (eds) (1997) *Opening the Nursery Door*, London: Routledge.

Minns, H. (1997) 'I knew a duck': reading and learning in Derby's poor schools, in *Opening the Nursery Door*. London: Routledge.

Mishra, R.C., Sinha, D. and Berry, J.W. (1996) *Ecology, Acculturation and Psychological Adaptation*. London: Sage Publications.

Rogoff, B. (1990) *Apprenticeship in Thinking: Cognitive Development in Social Context*. Oxford: Oxford University Press.

Rose, J. (2006) *An Independent Review of the Teaching of Early Reading*. Nottingham: DfES.

Spufford, M. (1997) Women teaching reading to poor children in the sixteenth and seventeenth centuries, in M. Hilton, M. Styles and V. Watson (eds) *Opening the Nursery Door*. London: Routledge.

Vincent, D. (1997) The domestic and the official curriculum in nineteenth-century England, in M. Hilton, M. Styles and V. Watson (eds) *Opening the Nursery Door*. London: Routledge.

Wells, G. (1986) *The Meaning Makers: Children Learning Language and Using Language to Learn*. Sevenoaks: Hodder and Stoughton.

Wood, D. (1988) *How Children Think and Learn*. Oxford: Blackwell.

3 Understanding educational discourse: attending to multiple voices

Kathy Goouch

Introduction

Babies and very young children have been characterized as watchers, listeners, puzzlers, problem solvers, symbolizers, creators, collaborators and players (David *et al.* 2003). All of this indicates that they are primed for learning from birth, are intrinsically motivated to explore and make meaning of their worlds, and that the families, communities and cultures in which they grow have primary influence on the learners they become and their first taste of the literate world. The intention of this chapter is to examine the case for using our knowledge of how children learn to be literate from birth to 3 in school contexts so that children can be supported in seamlessly progressing from emergent stages of literacy towards becoming full and critically literate participants in both an academic and social world. There are newly developing constraints on teachers and powerful lobbies who seek to limit and control young children's access to rich and empowering literacy practices and these too need to be examined and understood. At the beginning of this chapter some case study material of one child growing up in her literacy-rich world will be used to exemplify theory.

In this chapter there may not be new, unique or innovative ideas but there seems to be a burgeoning need to restate the findings of rigorously undertaken research now, in a worrying era, where flimsily supported political aims are being driven uncritically into the everyday lives of children, their teachers and their families.

Gabi's literacy world: the discourse of home literacy practices

Everybody talks to newborn babies. Gabi's mum and dad say hello and welcome her to the world; the midwives and nurses chatter to her. Gabi has already recognized her mother's voice (Karmiloff and Karmiloff-Smith 2001) and the tunes and patterns of her 'mother tongue' (Trevarthan 1998), and is listening and watching. Visitors, friends and family come and go and Gabi is surrounded by voices, by language, by faces. Her world is taking shape. As she is swapped between adults' welcoming arms, they and other children make eye contact with her, respond to her movements and wriggles, talk and sing to her and around her. Gabi is experiencing the world of human communication and social engagement and, because babies are 'tuned to enter the world of human action ... it is obvious that an enormous amount of the activity of the child during the first year and a half of life is extraordinarily social and communicative' (Bruner 1983: 27). Gabi is becoming 'attuned' to the languages of her home, which are culturally defined, and her learning will include words, sounds, intonation and the music of language, syntax, gesture, stories, songs and rhymes. Gabi has stories read at bedtime, board and soft books in her cot and in her pram, and she has waterproof books in her bath. On the walls of her bedroom are size charts, alphabet posters, nursery rhyme characters and a map of the world and she has grown up asking questions about the pictures around her. Her parents sing to her to keep her attention when changing her nappy and they all dance around when music is playing. By the age of one she imitates adult behaviour, picking up the hair brush and brushing her hair, pressing the buttons and holding the phone to her ear and chatting. She claps her hands to nursery rhymes and laughs gleefully at this kind of rhythmic play. She has an easel and chalk and makes marks and draws. Before the age of 2 she is able to use a pencil and wants to know what she has written. By the age of 3 she is writing pages of information, marks in lines across the page. She wants to know what print means, on road signs, in newspapers, on the television. Before the age of 4 she is helping to send birthday cards on the internet, as well as reading the pictures on favourite cereal boxes. Gabi has played on CBeebies on the internet until now she can navigate her way around it all on her own with no help from parents at all. Her mother writes:

> One day we went out for a walk and she decided to write down everything she saw on a piece of paper – I think she was just 4. She stopped every three steps to write down something else. She nearly caused an international incident when this piece of paper

blew out of her hands and across the road. A stranger stopped traffic to run and get it back. Gabi was absolutely distraught because her page of information which she'd spent so much time writing had gone. When the stranger got it back I think he was a bit confused as to why this page of scribbles was so important.

Much has been made of research demonstrating the abilities of newborn babies to imitate (see Meltzoff's protruding tongue experiments; Gopnik *et al.* 1999), although Vygotsky (1978) and Meltzoff (2004) confirm that imitation is a highly sophisticated act requiring 'the means of stepping from something one knows to something new' (Vygotsky 1978: 187) and so imitation is somewhat different to 'mimicry' (David *et al.* 2003). Such imitations are also likely to occur within safe and familiar contexts and in the company of safe and familiar carers. So, Gabi and her mum engage in intimate conversations, with Gabi often initiating these and drawing attention to herself and her developing 'voice', and her mum eager to respond; they imitate each other. In these ways Gabi's conscious mind is developing and her experience of language and literacy events is growing in such early conversations and family activity. Talk events occur in and around everyday routines – feeding, bathing, nappy changing, dressing and undressing – with naming and conversing, influencing Gabi's emerging vocabulary. Quite painlessly and in the company of her family, Gabi becomes involved in naming the world and, as Greenfield reminds us, 'minds develop as brains do – as an individual starts to escape genetic programming in favour of personal experience-based learning' (Greenfield 2000a: 181).

Gabi is learning an enormous amount from her home context: she is learning the status of language from the noise and voices of her family and friends; the value of intimate conversations and the importance of close interactions. She is also learning about the status of conventional literacy and multi-modal texts. Stories are told and read and meaningful print is mediated for her. The world of response to story is unfolded in facial, body and oral expressions. As she begins to crawl and can identify her floor-based book stand, she is already making choices and sometimes conforming to the choices of others; she is expressing her will in her insistence on certain texts and her choices are valued.

At all stages, Gabi is performing within the frame that her family and the local society sets for her; that is, print and talk is a reality of her life, therefore she engages with the same resources for the same purposes and with the same intentions and commitment as her parents and family. She becomes confident and eager to participate, relaxed and able to opt in or out at will. She develops her own purposes for literacy ... signs and notices, invitations, or just writing, making marks that express meaning or matter to her in some, often unidentified, way. Gabi is learning to be literate because it matters to her to do so. She will continue to learn because it serves her social and cognitive purposes. Language and literacy events have already been satisfying and enjoyable for her; they have already served to further her own ends, to meet her needs, to help her to express herself, to understand and to be understood. For Gabi, becoming confident, developing a strong sense of self-esteem, developing a sense of self in relation to the world, occurs in a safe and supported family context. It is here that issues of identity, a developing personality, are first recognized, then grown and confirmed safely, before school.

Importantly, what Gabi has learned about language, literacy, herself, her family and her world have all been learned in a context; this vast range of learning that has occurred from birth to 3 has all been situated and so she has been able to map new information and understanding together with existing knowledge safely, in known texts and in human contexts. Of course, Dewey, a century ago, was clear about the importance of human experience in school learning:

> From the standpoint of the child, the great waste in the school comes from his inability to utilize the experiences he gets outside the school in any complete and free way within the school itself; while on the other hand he is unable to apply in daily life what he is learning at school. When the child gets into the schoolroom he has to put out of his mind a large part of the ideas, interests and activities that predominate in his home and neighbourhood.
>
> (Dewey 1899: 75)

and he called for an 'organic connection' between the school and the everyday life of the child.

Gabi is now 4 and so of course she must go to school. Even though not of statutory school age, the social pressures and economic concerns of schools make it appear essential that she conforms to social norms and begins formal schooling at least a year before statutory school age. Her contemporaries in other European countries are playing in kindergartens and engaging in informal learning contexts with teachers specifically trained in the phase. While the majority of Gabi's day is still spent informally, making choices in relation to social groupings and activities, engaging in intimate conversations, storying herself and being told and read stories, sometimes Gabi also has to perform directed school literacy tasks. For example, she is required to demonstrate that she knows the 'W'ness of W by filling in worksheets and drawing objects she knows with that initial sound. It is on this that she is being formally assessed, rather than her joy in story, her ability to retell favourite tales and her very positive attitude to reading and writing, all of which are much harder to measure. Needless to say, her competence in using computer technology for communicative purposes and her interest in screen literacy is not being acknowledged. Nevertheless, her early school experience is largely positive, is building on early learning contexts, is informal and playful and has not dented her sense of self as a reader, her confidence or her developing knowledge of what counts as important in literacy. Gabi is fortunate and her teacher is unusual. However, it is not certain how long she will be able to maintain a healthy, child-focused context and curriculum with current pressures to narrow literacy learning in the early years of schooling.

Where are we now?

Understanding how children think, develop and learn in order to carefully inform educational practices depends on access to many fields of enquiry: for example, developmental and cognitive psychology, new neuroscience, sociology and new socio-cultural theories, philosophy and theories of the nature of knowledge – as well as educational theories from research. In the last 25 years, at least, research – at international level, cross-national, national, local and school-based levels – has been carried out rigorously to inform how we nurture and support children in school contexts as they make sense of the literacy practices already encountered and the new skills introduced to them. The social nature of literacy, the importance of cultural practices has been highlighted by international anthropological work reported in detail (Brice Heath 1983; Street 1984) as well as other work more recently promoting a socio-cultural approach to teaching and learning (Lankshear 1997, Hall 2003). Neuroscientists have recently pointed to the significance of, for example, environments in promoting development (Greenfield 2000a) and developmental psychologists have, over decades, focused upon 'significant others' and relationships between adults and learners in learning contexts (Vygotsky 1978).

Improbably, then, educators working in England find themselves facing political pressure to comply in 'delivering' a single phonics package to all children as the 'first, fast and only' approach to the teaching of reading. New policies are adopting a 'simple view of reading' (DfES 2006). As usual, in politically driven initiatives, there seems to be an emphasis on expedience, fast-tracking children through programmes which, it is assumed, provide them with basic literacy skills.

The language of power: the political world of education and educational discourse

There is a duality of language employed in the discourse which is being used to drive such strong political messages home: the first is of 'common sense' – that is, there is a common assumption that everybody understands that, in Western Europe, language is represented by a symbolic alphabetic system and clearly all children need to *know* this in order to decode and encode language. This is what many believe is the total of what is needed to read and write. Indeed, a recent Secretary of State for Education made a very bold attempt to create division between educational research and the practice it intended to inform:

> Some researchers are so obsessed with 'critique', so out of touch with reality that they churn out findings which no one with the slightest common sense could take seriously.
>
> (Blunkett 1999, in Pring 2004: 218)

This kind of appeal to mass opinion, including teachers who are clearly in touch with 'reality', is an example of the political will to erode confidence in anything other than central policies.

The second language is of targets and levels and the word 'systematic' is constantly employed, appealing again to a popular notion that reading and writing can be taught in incremental units. Indeed, it is almost ten years now since Cathy Nutbrown examined what, at that time, was a developing educational discourse (Nutbrown 1998: 17), arguing that new language in the education field – of 'battle, managerialism and competition' – used terms such as 'orders, standards, levels, stages, targets and outcomes'. In her paper, Nutbrown further asserts that

> conversations that value children's achievements and positive discourses in early childhood are *impossible* (her italics) without words like development, exploration, facilitation, response, support, interest, investigation and growth, and writings and documents that omit such words should be regarded with suspicion.
>
> (1998: 17)

It would be challenging now to find educators brave enough to use such language aloud without themselves arousing suspicion.

Of course, language is not devoid of attachment to meaning, cannot be neutral and must be understood in the context in which it is used, that is, the historical, social and political context. And so, since 1998, even more new attitudes, new systems, new constructs of schooling and education and new layers of discourse have emerged. Alexander talks of the

> strutting machismo of standards, targets, step changes, league tables, task forces, best practice and failing schools, and the endless parade (or 'rolling out') of initiatives and strategies, each habitually but implausibly prefaced by 'tough' or 'new', or more commonly both.
>
> (Alexander 2007: 194)

New political dominance of education policies appears to be reflecting a broader surge towards globalization which is 'promoting particular values that are supportive of consumerism and capital accumulation' (Olsson *et al.* 2004: 6) and hence the new hierarchy of discourse. Acknowledging how closely education and schooling are politically entwined may be the key to understanding why skills training in functional forms of literacy has become such a major political imperative:

> Those who want researchers to cut the theory and simply to say 'what works' forget that what counts as 'working' makes many unquestioned assumptions which need to be examined.
>
> Pring 2004: 220)

There are, of course, many dangers in openly examining what it is that has status in a national curriculum, in a democratic society. It would become possible then to question the instrumental nature of schooling; the pressure of economics on educational visions; ideas about value for money; the short-term notions of what counts as 'effective' in schools; 'what works'; the faults in evaluative tools used to measure standards, and more. It seems unlikely that the recent, centrally funded and government-supported *Independent Review of the Teaching of Early Reading* (Rose 2006) could in any way be as 'independent' as claimed. As Apple suggests, it is necessary to understand 'the larger social context in which the current politics of official knowledge generates' (Apple 1997: 596). He continues: 'Powerful groups ... have been able to redefine the terms of debates in education ... what education is for is being transformed' (1997: 596). Apple suggests that rather than being part of a 'social alliance ... acting to propose social democratic policies for schools, expanding educational opportunities', a new alliance exists which now 'aims at providing the educational conditions believed necessary ... for increasing international competitiveness, profit, and discipline' (Apple 1997: 596). In her examination of contemporary education policy, Hall calls to attention Prime Minister's plan for education in creating a 'culture of enterprise', signifying current political impulses to identify and understand 'knowledge' simply for 'application and exploitation, especially and significantly, for wealth creation' (Hall 2004: 10). Enshrined within educational discourse now are new terms: 'knowledge economy', 'knowledge societies', 'knowledge revolution' and, of course, 'knowledge transfer', all assuming common understanding and common acceptance that the nature of 'knowledge' is understood, that it has been revolutionized, marketized and can be easily transferred.

Understanding what counts as 'knowledge' in schools now, and where and in whose interests such decisions are made, is important in the context of policies relating to the teaching of reading. The attraction of breaking the rather complex and sophisticated process called 'reading' into simply acquired, hierarchical skills is partly because 'it fits in well with general cultural moves towards measuring and monitoring human activities' (Barton 1994: 162). In this way, then, as well as controlling what counts as knowledge and measuring and monitoring the development of children and learners, the resources and materials encountered by young readers can also be controlled to fit in with an easy to understand and easy to manage teaching method.

This reductionist view of how children learn to read and to be literate, the idea that it can be simply broken down into steps or skills to be learned, has been proliferated around the margins of educational practice for some time. It is periodically resurrected whenever there is a perceived crisis in reading 'standards', which happens at regular, politically sensitive moments, and when popular opinion can be harnessed in support of those propagating the message. Understanding what can be gained from redefining reading into discrete stages will help in addressing misconceptions. First, if, as some psychologists in particular believe, and as the 'simple view of reading' (Rose 2006) would suggest, reading can be taught as a set of separately learned 'skills', then any suggestion that reading is a complex process to be understood and taught by *teachers* is dispelled – anyone can encourage children to chant the alphabet and memorize symbols on flash cards, and so an economic purpose may be detected here. Secondly, if children are to be instructed in detecting sounds and symbols, then this is easily measurable, targets easily set, and so called standards easily achieved, thus fulfilling loudly claimed political aims. Thirdly, very large commercial interests are now involved in producing educational material and there is certainly much to be gained by some publishers of both commercial schemes and the new 'decodable books' (Rose 2006: 82) from which Rose claims there is much to be gained. Of course, 'skills' are also closely connected to ideas of 'functional literacy' and, 'using skills often suggests you can abstract some neutral techniques which people possess, located somewhere inside the person, which are the same across all situations, and which can be added to piecemeal, (Barton 1994: 165). In all cases, notions of 'expertness' are removed from the teaching professional and what counts as success is very much reduced.

The language now used to describe the teaching of reading: 'quick wins', 'rapidity' and 'covering ground' (Rose 2006) is ill fitting when we remember that it refers to how very young children like Gabi are learning to use communicative systems and symbols, complex in themselves and representing the complexities of a changing world into which they are growing. The idea of 'quick wins' does not suggest the possibility of sustained or embedded learning which is important as young children integrate new skills, interests and practices into early learned reading practices. In the company of colleagues, policy makers, politicians and parents, it feels bold now, if not downright subversive, to claim that children (or indeed 'people') might not learn, acquire knowledge or skills in straightforward incremental ways, or 'systematically', as is often assumed. Instead, learning, including learning to read and write, may appear messy with young learners going forwards, sideways and sometimes back before they fit new learning into the puzzling and sometimes contradictory world in which they live and grow.

Whatever professionals, politicians or policy makers *think*, it is imperative to remember that, whichever policy is conceived and implemented in literacy education, it will affect children's life chances, their attitudes to any future learning, their ability to make and critically shape their worlds and thus, ultimately, the advancement of the society in which we live. The 'simple' task of educationalists, then, is to know and understand the range of theories across disciplines that may inform teaching and learning, to understand multiple discourses, and then, authoritatively, translate it into a common language that can be accepted by all and understood in policy terms in order to maximize children's potential to critically understand words and worlds. It is only in this way that understanding can lead development and practice for the benefit of Gabi and her peers and transcend political will, individuals' ambitions and commercial interests.

Phonics: a naïve and commercially distorted world

The idea that there may be political and commercial interests in forefronting a single approach to teaching literacy, and specifically phonics, has already been identified in this chapter. 'Common-sense' notions of what counts as knowledge in reading relate only in this new order to alphabetic knowledge and, currently, synthetic phonics. However, there is naïve simplicity in any approach that attempts to induct young children into reading and literacy through an instructional approach relying only in the first instance on individual, decontextualized phonemes. This has been consistently projected as the only 'common-sense' approach, now required to be the 'first, fast and only' approach to teaching reading, in spite of research findings and alternative views that strongly reject it as neither appropriate nor successful, and in spite of the real 'common-sense' approach to early literacy taken by many parents similar to Gabi's.

Of course, definitions of what constitutes 'reading' also differ; professional and educational discourse defines reading as complex and incorporating 'performances of meaning' (Bruner 1986) as the reader brings experience, understanding and personal interest to a text. Others simply define reading as 'decoding' print, a significantly limited aspect of a much broader concept; a small and often insignificant part of a much more substantial whole. Those that propose limiting the teaching of reading in the early years to phonic instruction, and specifically synthetic phonics instruction, appear to assume that children themselves will make connections between what is provided in instructional phonics sessions and other literacy events involving connected texts. This would require an enormous leap of understanding on the part of small children, who have been accustomed like Gabi to learning in familiar, context-driven activities. And, of course, this would be an even larger leap for those children who have had little or no mediated support in literacy before school. However, in other fields of scientific knowledge, in other disciplines, which sometimes carry more weight than educational theories, there is information to support a significantly broader approach. Further, there is evidence to suggest that meaning and personal connections are crucial to learning:

> The brain is not merely a great transmitter, a super switch-board, it is better likened to a great transformer. The current of experience that passes through it undergoes a change of character not through ... the sense by which the perception entered but by virtue of a primary use which is made of it

immediately. It is sucked into the stream of symbols which constitute a human mind.

(Langer 1951 in Robinson 2001: 127)

Rather than any information given to the child, in the form of phonic instruction, for example, having a direct impact on the brain and therefore on learning, this suggests that there is an 'intermediate' process when human sense needs to be made of it. More recent work by neuroscientists supports this theory:

It is now well established that visual signals are not just relayed passively into the deep recesses of the brain and up into the cortex. Instead there are also other connections that intercept this incoming stream of information, projecting it back down in the opposite direction to modify the way the incoming signal is relayed and thus how the world is perceived. We see the world in terms of what we have seen already.

(Greenfield 2000a: 65)

It seems that the personal meaning which learners overlay and integrate with new information is essential for both development and learning. Everything, 'facts and contexts' (Greenfield 2000a: 65), needs to be contextualized for learning. Just as Gabi learned that sounds and words carried meaning and made sense in her own life from very early beginnings both orally and in print, so does she need to be able to find ways of making 'W' fit into her already rapidly developing understanding of the symbolic world of language and literacy:

Making knowledge about language explicit, standing back from the functions and forms of writing and focusing on the ways language and print 'work' makes so much more sense if the writing is embedded in a context which makes sense to the child ... 'Goldilocks and the Three Bears' will be easier to understand than 'b'. The word 'bear' and then perhaps the letter 'b' can however be examined, recognized and understood as part of this favourite text. Words and letters can then be taken to other texts.'

(Martin and Leather 1994: 31)

Intuitively, many parents, carers and families engage constantly in this kind of contextualizing practice, darting back and forth between previously shared experiences and new learning and developing memory along with new connections. Brains, it seems, develop and grow, shaping the mind by 'enhancing each conscious moment by imbuing each snapshot of the outside world with meaning' (Greenfield 2000a: 164). Since there appears now to be so much evidence that meaning and experience, contexts and environments contribute so fully to learning, then the early years literacy curriculum and the role of teaching professionals needs to be very carefully considered. As Dewey warned more than a century ago, 'the unity of education is dissipated, and studies become centrifugal; so much of this study to secure this end, so much of that to secure another, until the whole becomes a sheer compromise and patchwork between contending aims and disparate studies' (Dewey [1889] 1915: 72). Given such patchworks, which have been increased many times over in the intervening years, it is incredible that young children make any sense of schooling and 'school literacy' at all, let alone the 75 per cent of successful early readers that Rose ignores in his Review (2006).

And so to school and a new discourse . . .

For most young children beginning school, there is an enormous bridge to cross between home practices generally and expectations of school. And, for some, the bridge will not exist at all if experiences at home are distant from school practices. For example, being confined to one room for much of the day presents a very real challenge to children who have been used to moving around their home freely. Sitting still, in any position, cross-legged on the floor or on a chair at a table, for any length of time again will appear strange to most and will present physical challenges to some children. To combine these artificial requirements, in artificial surroundings, with the task of performing decontextualized phonic activities for no observable purpose will perhaps serve only to confuse or mislead some young children about the functions and forms of language and literacy and the functions of school. Many children, like Gabi, will have already begun to enjoy, engage with, and succeed in purposeful and meaningful literacy events in and around their home and family. 'School literacy' will then appear as a different act. Just as school children are often confused when they are asked for a 'reading book', worrying about whether it should be their scheme book or a book of choice, so they will become confused about what constitutes literacy practice; is it reading and writing for meaning, for information, for interest, for joy or is it when they chant sounds and decode words? For other children, not familiar with literacy practices valued by school, 'school literacy' will appear even more distant from any existing experience of print and literacy they may have encountered before and outside school (Brice Heath 1983). For many young children, then, making sounds aloud to match letters will be a strange activity, not connected or able to be connected with prior knowledge or experience. Rather strangely, Rose is satisfied that 'barking at print' is a stage that young children need to pass through to become competent readers (Rose 2006: 20) and, again strangely, likens this to competent adults 'barking at print' with unfamiliar text. Of course, competent adult readers always have a range of semantic and syntactic information to draw on and rarely, if ever, can be heard to 'bark' through even the most complex of texts. If teaching reading becomes synonymous with phonics instruction then it is difficult to see how young children will make sense of this activity, create connections with other real literacy experiences, make analogous connections with print experienced elsewhere and become both proficient and committed readers, rather than simply functional decoders of print. But perhaps that is all that is required of young readers; not that reading should be a critical, discerning and analytical act as Freire describes:

> Reading does not consist merely of decoding the written word or language; rather it is preceded by and intertwined with knowledge of the world. Language and reality are dynamically interconnected. The understanding attained by critical reading of a text implies perceiving the relationship between text and context.
>
> (Freire and Macedo 1987: 29)

The 'word–world' connectedness that Freire describes is imperative in supporting early developing readers, and writers, like Gabi who already have, and importantly *know* that they have, an enormous amount of information about how texts work. They need this information to be both acknowledged and extended rather than shattered by narrow school practices. Creating greater disconnections, discontinuity, between home and school, instead of bridging the two big experiences in children's lives, cannot hope to serve young children well.

Professional discourse: multilingual practices

Effective teachers of literacy have already been found to be those who 'tended to teach letter sounds within the context of using a text' (Medwell *et al.* 1998) and Hall develops this by suggesting that pedagogy matters to 'good' teachers of reading, who will:

- understand children as 'intentional' beings;
- understand learning as a 'volitional' process;
- see themselves as powerful enablers;
- connect context and environment with learning to read;
- adapt resources and environment to suit individual learners.

(Hall 2006: 19, 20)

The importance of this level of subject knowledge of literacy teachers, pedagogical knowledge in relation to literacy, is yet to be emphasized in this round of the debate. In the early years of schooling particularly, understanding children's intentionality is crucial in supporting them in making links between this and any additional information they need to engage in communicative acts. Acknowledging and forefronting children's intentions will inevitably result in close engagement of young learners in reading and in affective literacy events. So that, just as reading and writing, for example, party invitations at home, writing notes on the fridge, highlighting programmes in television guides, knowing what advertisements on hoardings or on the side of buses are persuading us to buy, and reading titles and credits on favourite television programmes all seriously *matter* to children, so it is also possible to create reading contexts in school that matter equally. In this way, children can be encouraged to orchestrate all of their developing knowledge of the way that print works in order to find out where the meaning lies, and will be motivated to do so. Indeed, Ofsted, in their own evaluation of the teaching of reading in primary schools, identified some schools as ineffective when they failed to build on 'children's own reading interests and the range of reading material they read outside school' (Ofsted 2004: 4).

One of the 'main ingredients for success in the teaching of beginner readers' is a 'well trained teaching force' ... and 'the quality of phonic work relies on the expertise, understanding and commitment of those who teach it' (Rose 2006: 7). Fortunately, what a 'well trained teaching force' might look like may still be beyond the reach of politicians and policy makers. If, as Nias claims, teachers' 'substantial self, a set of self-defining beliefs, values and attitudes, develops alongside situational selves, and is highly resistant to change' (Nias 1989: 203), then there is hope that new political whims will not sweep aside sound professional judgement based upon deeply held core values. What may be understood by the term 'well trained' could be worrying if, in new systems, as Hall suggests, there is 'a whole set of gateways through which would-be teachers are allowed to pass only if they are sufficiently conformist and accepting of their new technicist role' (Hall 2004: 2). Hall describes such teachers as 'restricted professionals' who lack a wider vision of their role and who have taken on board a 'technical–rational–implementational approach to their work' (48), which may well become more commonly the case as central government prescriptions become common practice, impacting on young professionals starting out in schools as well as those already struggling to make human sense of the politics of literacy teaching.

How teachers view themselves in their role as reading teachers is important. In research they have been understood to be involved in 'a complex and highly skilled activity which holds in balance, and occasionally transcends, the historical, sociological, philosophical, psychological and practical tensions and constraints of the work itself' and with their teaching understood 'as a craft and sometimes as an art' (Nias 1989: 201). In policy documents such highly skilled activities in relation to teaching developing readers have been reduced to 'work ... that may not be rocket science' (Rose 2007: 6).

What should teachers be trained to do or to be and with which discourse should they engage? In reviewing this, ideas in relation to 'dominant discourse regimes' have a particular resonance:

> Such regimes of truth make assumptions and values invisible; they turn subjective perspectives and understandings into apparently objective realities; and they determine some things to be self-evident and realistic while others appear to make no sense and are obviously impractical. In other words, they are means by which the ethical and political are transformed into the technical and managerial.
>
> (Dahlburg and Moss 2005: 142)

It is not difficult to find in current curriculum policy documents phrases such as 'it is generally understood that ...', 'obviously ...', 'it is widely agreed that ...', 'virtually all have agreed that ...' (see, for example, Rose 2006) without reference to contributors to such statements. Perhaps, as Dahlburg and Moss claim, this kind of discursive ploy serves to 'shape what we think, how we talk and in what ways we act ... (serving) a disciplinary or regulatory function' (142). The tight focus currently on didactic practices, on instruction, has also led to some rather specific, if torturous, language in the requirement for teachers to engage children in '*instructive learning play* environments' (Rose 2006: 105), perhaps hoping to touch base with all corners of the debate by including these three somewhat contradictory adjectives in the same statement. Of course, children may learn while they play and some play may be instructive, but Rose's phrasing sounds suspiciously more prescriptive than this.

If Gabi and her family is representative at all, they represent families who help their children to master literacy skills that are useful to them at the time when they need to use them and for their own purposes. They also represent members of society who expect the education system to which they subscribe to acknowledge Gabi's knowledge of words and worlds, celebrate her successes, help her to achieve her self-set goals and extend these. Her teachers then need to seek to understand her, her cultural context, the world in which she is growing and developing, her desires, her interests and what motivates her. In tandem with this array of knowledge, her teachers also need to understand how children in general develop as readers, which texts will help Gabi to read, as well as institutional and government expectations. It is this 'pedagogic balancing' (Nias 1989) that moves teaching away from technicist activities and further towards the 'rocket science' involved in professional practice. Children need teachers who will understand, as Hall explains, that learning to read is rather more than 'barking at print':

> New, socio-cultural perspectives on our understandings of literacy see children not as mastering school literacy practices (or any school practice for that matter) without being motivated to enter into and identify with that practice, and without believing that they will be able to function within it and use it in the here and now of their lives.
>
> (Hall 2004: 55)

This view, of course, creates a new discourse and places education beyond mere instrumentalism, assumes success rather than failure, assumes relevance rather than decontextualized activity and assumes that children's intentions are important. Shaping pedagogy around these rather simple ideas could conceivably improve children's interest in and attitudes towards reading practices in school. In the justification for a Review of Primary Education, Alexander claims that 'educational quality and standards are culturally, philosophically, and indeed empirically much more complex notions than their political arbiters admit' (Alexander 2007: 194) and it is an understanding of this complexity by all concerned that all children deserve in their childhood experiences of school education. We need also to be reminded that 'political vision is notoriously short-term' and that 'educational vision cannot afford to be'. Let us hope that, in Gabi's early days at school, her teacher has sufficient professional freedom to take time to recognize that Gabi can write information texts, navigate the CBeebies site, find England on the map of the world, sing along with lots of songs learned from children's television, and that she has a strongly developing phonological awareness, has lots of favourite books and stories and recognizes letters in her name. The danger is that the letters in Gabi's name will not be in the initial list of sounds that her teacher is being told to teach her when she first gets to school.

References

Alexander, R. (2007) Where there is no vision ... *Forum*, 49 (1): 187–99.

Apple, M.W. (1997) What postmodernists forget: cultural capital and official knowledge in A.H. Halsey, H. Lander, P. Brown and A.S. Wells (eds) *Education, Culture Economy Society*. Oxford: Oxford University Press.

Ball, S. (ed.) (2004) *The RoutledgeFalmer Reader in Sociology of Education*. London: RoutledgeFalmer.

Barton, D. (1994) *Literacy: An Introduction to the Ecology of Written Language*. Oxford: Blackwell.

Brice Heath, S. (1983) *Ways with Words*. Cambridge: Cambridge University Press.

Bruner, J. (1983) *Child's Talk: Learning to Use Language*. Oxford: Oxford University Press.

Bruner, J. (1986) *Actual Minds, Possible Worlds*. Cambridge, MA: Harvard University Press.

Dahlburg, G., Moss, P. and Pence, A. (1999) *Beyond Quality in Early Childhood Education and Care: Postmodern Perspectives*. London: RoutledgeFalmer.

Dahlburg, G. and Moss, P. (2005) *Ethics and Politics in Early Childhood Education*. London: RoutledgeFalmer.

David, T., Goouch, K., Powell, S. and Abbott, L. (2003) *Birth to Three Matters: A Review of the Literature*. London: DfES.

Dewey, J. ([1889] 1915) *The School and Society*, 2nd edition. Chicago, IL: University of Chicago Press.

DfES (Department for Education and Science) (2006) *The Primary National Strategy*. London: DfES.

Freire, P. and Macedo, D. (1987) *Literacy: Reading the Word and the World*. London: Routledge.

Gopnik, A., Melzoff, A. and Kuhl, P. (1999) *How Babies Think: The Science of Childhood*. London: Weidenfeld and Nicolson.

Greenfield, S. (2000a) *The Private Life of the Brain*. London: Penguin.

Greenfield, S. (2000b) *Brain Story*. London: BBC Publications.

Hall, K. (2003) *Listening to Stephen Read: Multiple Perspectives on Literacy*. Buckingham: Open University Press.

Hall, K. (2004) *Literacy and Schooling: Towards Renewal in Primary Education Policy*. Aldershot: Ashgate.

Hall, K. (2006) How children learn to read and how phonics helps, in M. Lewis and S. Ellis (eds) *Phonics Practice, Research and Policy*. London: UKLA/PCP.

Karmiloff, K. and Karmiloff-Smith, A. (2001) *Pathways to Language: From Fetus to Adolescent*. Cambridge, MA: Harvard University Press.

Lankshear, C. (1997) *Changing Literacies*. Buckingham: Open University Press.

Martin, T. and Leather, B. (1994) *Readers and Texts in the Primary Years*. Buckingham: Open University Press.

Medwell, J., Wray, D., Poulson, L. and Fox, R. (1998) *Effective Teachers of Literacy*. Exeter: University of Exeter.

Meltzoff, A. (2004) Imitation as a mechanism of social cognition: origins of empathy, theory of mind and the representation of action, in U. Goswami (ed.) *Childhood Cognitive Development*. Oxford: Blackwell.

Nias, J. (1989) *Primary Teachers Talking: A Study of Teaching as Work*. London: Routledge.

Nutbrown, C. (1998) *The Lore and Language of Early Education*. Sheffield: USDE.

Ofsted (Office for Standards in Education) (2004) *Reading for Purpose and Pleasure*. London: Ofsted.

Olssen, M., Codd, H. and O'Neill, A.M. (2004) *Education Policy: Globalization, Citizenship and Democracy*. London: Sage Publications.

Pring, R. (2004) *Philosophy of Education, Aims, Theory, Common Sense and Research*. London: Continuum.

Robinson, K. (2001) *Out of Our Minds: Learning to be Creative*. Oxford: Capstone.

Rose, J. (2006) *An Independent Review of the Teaching of Early Reading*. Nottingham: DfES.

Street, B.V. (1984) *Literacy in Theory and Practice*. Cambridge: Cambridge University Press.

Trevarthan, C. (1998) The child's need to learn a culture, in M. Woodhead, D. Faulkner and K. Littleton (eds) *Cultural Worlds of Early Childhood*. London: Routledge/Open University Press.

Vygotsky, L.S. (1978) *Mind in Society: The Development of Higher Psychological Processes*. Cambridge, MA: Harvard University Press.

4   The limits of science in the phonics debate

Patrick Shannon

On 24 August 2007 approximately 2500 members of the International Astronomical Union (IAU) voted that Pluto wasn't a planet any longer. Discovered in 1930 by the American astronomer Clyde Tombaugh, recently Pluto had fallen on hard times because it was discovered to lack a roundish shape, to overlap the orbit of Neptune, and to be smaller than other non-planet objects in the solar system. It is an ice ball and not a rock ball or gaseous giant like the other still-planets. Pluto did not go down without a fight, and several members of the IAU confessed that they were teary-eyed after the vote. The majority felt, however, that Pluto caused astronomy too many problems to retain its status. If it were to remain after the new discoveries became public, then 50 more objects in the solar system would have to be considered for planet status. Rather than add 50, IAU members felt it better to tighten the definition of planet a bit and lose one.

The fate of Pluto affords us a unique view of science. Pluto existed as a planet for nearly 80 years because of the scientific culture of instruments (Pluto can't be seen by the naked eye), scientists, and a particular cosmology. With a change of mind, but not of reality, Pluto ceased to exist as a planet. And the vote was not unanimous. Pluto did not explode or implode with the vote, but its meaning certainly did. Outside astronomy, Pluto is intelligible only within a framework and narrative of explanation that is associated, but not synonymous, with scientific understanding. Pluto has been embedded for nearly 80 years in professional definition of 'planetness' and, therefore, has occupied a featured place within textbooks and student aphorisms and mobiles. By raising their hands, the IAU changed the web of Pluto's scientific meaning and its social meaning as well. The reasons for that decision were based on human interests, and not some objective, natural or disinterested rationale. With that act, the IAU made the limits of science public, demonstrating that it is a rhetorical struggle to determine how people will act on and use the things that exist, rather than a discovery of natural laws and order.

In the United States, reading has suffered a fate similar to that of the solar system. No one disputes the existence of phonics. All theoretical and practical discussions of reading include statements about phonics, its reality and its definition. The webs of meaning in use that surround phonics are located in and draw significance from cultural and historical settings – even the scientific considerations of phonics. From time to time, collectives of people have come together to cast votes on the place of phonics within reading and the teaching of reading, and the consequences of those votes revolve around the relative power of the groups to command the field in reading education. This power is not limited to coercion through physical force; it also includes the rhetorical frames that capture the imagination and loyalties of participants in reading instruction. As with Pluto, the science and scientists of phonics perform this rhetorical struggle to determine how we will act on phonics and use it in American classrooms.

In what follows, I trace some of these struggles over phonics and science within American reading education during the last century. I begin with Edmond Burke Huey's *The Psychology and Pedagogy of Reading* [1908] 1968 and work through to the 2007 Presidential State of the Union Address. President Bush's declaration that No Child Left Behind (NCLB) should be reauthorized in 2007 'because it's working' is an official endorsement of the phonics-based reading instruction mandated in American schools since 2002. (NCLB is the current version of the 1965 Elementary and Secondary School Education Act, which established a federal presence in state-controlled public schools.) As all recent reports on the impact of NCLB attest, however, the President's endorsement and the evaluation are more political than scientific statements.

Some words about history

In 1992, Francis Fukuyama penned *The End of History and the Last Man*, a book in which he argued that the end of the Cold War signalled the end of the linear progression of human history. His premise was that the collapse of the Soviet Union represented the victory of Western liberal democracy over all other forms of government. His theoretical point of origin for this argument was that the antagonisms within the Master and Slave dialectic that Hegel posed at the beginning of the nineteenth century had been substantially resolved in the triumph of the world's democracies over the world's dictatorships. The spirit of freedom had finally been realized in the 1990s. Fukuyama based this claim upon what he considered to be irrefutable evidence – the governments in the majority of countries around the world characterized themselves as democracies, governments by the people. Because, at least in theory, democracies provide all individuals with the freedom to vote for who they hope will represent their interests in government, the Master and Slave can co-exist, if not live in complete harmony. In Fukuyama's view, a society's winners could lie down with its losers in order to form a citizenry secure in the knowledge that they participated in the system that brought about their government. In Hegelian terms, the purpose of history had been realized and, therefore, history had ended.

Fukuyama's end of history is not Armageddon. Rather, it is the end of the debate over political ideologies because anti-democracies in their many forms had been discredited as unproductive. In Fukuyama's end of history, the world's citizens had reached consensus that we have found the one best system of government – Western democracy. Whether or not Fukuyama is correct about the end of history, his use of Hegelian notions of history fit well with the unfolding of reading education in the United States over the twentieth century. For example, Nila Banton Smith's *American Reading Instruction* (1965), considered by many to be the official history of the field, provides a chronology of continuous progress from colonial times to the present. Its 'story' tells of American educators' search for the one best method that would bring universal literacy within the United States. The International Reading Association has kept this book in print since the 1960s, with most recent editions including updates by contemporary scholars. Perhaps without intention, Smith followed Hegel's notion of history as the continued progression toward the realization of that spirit of universal literacy. Reading scientists discovered laws of reading, learning and teaching; business produced the technology of instruction based on those laws; and governments supplied the system for delivery of literacy to the populace.

Although Smith and her subsequent editors did not foresee the end of this history for reading education, many current reading experts, the federal government and publishers proclaim that we have reached consensus within the field concerning how people read, how they learn to read and how reading should be taught. Most of these claims are based on the National Reading Panel report (2000) that decided that phonological knowledge, phonics, fluency, vocabulary and comprehension were the only scientifically verifiable components of reading. The reading wars are over, they declare, and all sides must harness their efforts behind the one best system. According to this logic, No Child Left Behind is the proper mechanism to coordinate all parties in these efforts by setting a timetable of 2014 to achieve universal literacy in the United States. President Bush believes this end of history should be celebrated.

> It so happens this is the fourth anniversary of when I signed the No Child Left Behind Act ... I remember when I was the Governor of Texas, there was a lot of debate about different types of curriculum, different ways to teach reading. You might remember these debates. They were full of all kinds of politics. The best way to cut through political debate is to measure. The best way to say, the program I'm using is working is because you're able to measure to determine whether or not it's working ... The system is working.
>
> (Bush 2006)

Huey and the real rationalization of reading instruction

Ignoring the theoretical work of William James and G. Stanley Hall and the praxis of Francis Parker, John Dewey and the women who taught in Quincy, MA schools and the Laboratory School at the University of Chicago, Edmund Burke Huey captured the research and political agenda for a century of educational science in one brief statement. 'After all we have thus far been content with trial and error, too often allowing publishers to be our jury, and a real rationalization of the process of inducing the child with the practice of reading has not been made' [1908] (1968: 9). By ridiculing trial-and-error methods and deference to textbooks in the classroom, Huey sought to reduce the role of teachers and publishers in future discussions of reading education. He completed his proposed hierarchy of authority by chastizing psychologists (the implied 'we:' in his statement) for acceding power to publishers. Finally, he identified psychologists as the only group capable of performing a real rationalization of reading and instruction and, therefore, the primary group to assume authority over scientifically managed reading instruction. Psychologists would develop true understanding of reading and the teaching of reading by subjecting both to scientific scrutiny. Through basic and applied research, psychologists would formulate the guiding principles for both curriculum and instruction. Publishers would translate the principles into technology for classroom use, and then teachers would implement the technology.

The National Society for the Study of Education (NSSE) was among the first to take up Huey's challenge, by appointing a Committee for the

Economy of Time in Education in 1911. This group was charged with translating Fredrick W. Taylor's system for the standardization of production from industry to schools. Standardization was to be accomplished by dividing the production into its elemental parts, measuring the efficiency and effectiveness of each movement, and then coordinating those movements into the most productive flow by listing the steps of each task on an instructional card that workers were to follow. William S. Gray, Ernest Horn, James Fleming Hosic and E. L. Thorndike, among others, began by surveying existing curriculum and practices and subjecting each aspect to the equivalent of time and motion studies in order to determine which led to the greatest gain on the crude standardized measures available at that time. As participant Harold Rugg would later report, this work was an orgy of numbers that William S. Gray translated into 48 principles of reading instruction for the Committee's fourth report (1919). Gray concluded that it was nearly impossible to compare methods of instruction because the variability of effectiveness and efficiency of teachers within methods was at least as great as the differences among methods. A real rationalization of reading instruction, then, would await technological mediation in which within-method variation could be reduced significantly.

In 1918, the NSSE formed the Committee on Materials in Education by combining the Committee on the Measurement of Educational Products and the Committee on the Economy of Time in Education. 'At this point, the Society assigned to the present Committee the task of embodying, in concrete materials to be used in classrooms, the principles arrived at by the earlier committees' (Bagley 1920). To be certain, the reading textbooks of the 1920s began to incorporate principles from Gray's list – more emphasis on silent reading in upper grades, fewer multisyllabic words in early readers, more repetition of vocabulary across lessons – but the most significant changes were the expansion of teachers' guides and the use of a single textbook series across elementary school grades. Prior to the 1920s, it was common practice to use multiple series within and across grades within a school, presenting students with several sets of vocabulary and rules to learn. Moreover, publishers gave few directions on how to use their books – sometimes a single paragraph or page of general instructions were offered. Within the decade, all series included separate teachers' manuals ranging from 200 to 400 pages in length, with explicit language for teachers to follow and use during lessons.

Gray became a co-author of Elson readers (later Scott Foresman Dick and Jane series) in 1930. Under his direction, this basal reading series developed a near-monopoly within the field, controlling over 80 per cent of the market and directing most of the competing series to ape its content and format. Within these materials, phonics was defined as a whole-to-part process in which word recognition preceded and directed students' attention to individual letter/sound relationships. Surveys during the early 1960s found that teacher guidebooks directed instruction in 'almost every [school] system' (Austin and Morrison 1963) and that research and opinions of a very few people directed the field of reading education (Barton and Wilder 1964).

Jeanne Chall and the First Grade Studies

Following the launching of Sputnik in 1957, Congress passed the National Defense Education Act, which provided substantial funding to improve science and engineering education and acknowledged that American schools in general needed reform, if the United States was to win the Cold War. At that time, the National Conference of Research in English established a special committee on reading in order to reform reading education (Guy Bond, Jeanne Chall, Theodore Clymer, Donald Durrell, William Sheldon, Joseph Soffetti, Ralph Staiger and Russell Stauffer). That committee decided upon a two-pronged approach. Jeanne Chall would conduct a reinterpretation of existing research on reading instruction (funded by the Carnegie Foundation) and other committee members would begin a large-scale cooperative experiment with clearly defined goals that could provide solid evidence on which method of teaching reading brought the best results (funded by the Cooperative Research Branch of the US Office of Education). Of the 76 applications, 27 projects were selected to compare a variety of experimental curricula against existing basal reading series (with studies directed by J. Chall, E. Fry, A. Harris, A. Heilman, H. Murphy, R. Ruddell, G. Spache and others). Twenty-one of the directors were from universities, five from state departments of education and one from a school district.

When the studies ended, the coordinators of the project concluded that 'reading programs are not equally effective in all situations' because a successful treatment in one setting achieved poor results in another (Bond and Dykstra 1967: 428). Although most innovative combinations of basal reading series with phonics instruction appeared to be superior to the basal series alone, no combination was found to be effective in all situations. In sum, these researchers of the First Grade Studies concluded that there was no one best way to teach young children to read. From her review of existing research literature, Chall concurred that no single best method could be specified, but she was much more forceful in her endorsement of phonics: 'School systems can improve reading standards by using one of the complete code-emphasis programs or a separate supplemental phonics program as a replacement for the word-perception program in the conventional basal reading series' (Chall 1967: 310).

Although unable to determine the one best system of reading, these studies and Chall's review of literature enhanced the position of synthetic phonics in which instruction on letters and sound would precede word recognition. No one found phonics alone to be the solution to universal literacy, but many found that part-to-whole phonics improved the efficiency and effectiveness of early instruction. Along with evaluation procedures for Projects Head Start and Follow Through, the First Grade Studies helped to instantiate scores on standardized tests as the primary criterion for judging the success of a particular method or programme. The ambivalent results of the First Grade Studies did not provide the market conditions for publishers to make major changes within their programmes. As Chall would report over the next decades, the rhetoric within basal materials would change, but the whole-to-part orientation of their approach to beginning reading would remain unaltered.

> We have guidelines concerning the accuracy of our research. Most of us rely on a statistical significance of 5 per cent or 1 per cent to indicate that our findings occurred not from chance alone. But we seem not to have guidelines for turning research findings to guides for practice. How much research evidence is needed to turn our research findings into recommendations for practice? Should we rely on the standards of individual researchers, or do we need some common guidelines? How many confirmations of the First Grade Studies do we need before we put its findings to use?
>
> (Chall 1999: 9–10)

Fifteen years of National Reading Reports

Between 1985 and 2000, the federal government commissioned four state-of-the-science reports on reading in order to inform public policy, curriculum and instruction. Although the funding agencies varied slightly among the four reports, the pattern of their development and composition were identical. Government officials within the educational bureaucracy subcontracted the report to members of hand-picked committees to oversee the gathering, analysis and reporting of existing research studies. The committees and report writers were not directed on what to conclude or how to deliver those conclusions in any of these reports, but National Reading Panel member S. J. Samuels's statement at the International Reading Association Convention in Chicago (2006) cautioned:

> The areas of focus and the methods of analyses were decided by who was selected to the panel. The five areas of emphasis in the report do not capture all there is to reading. Rather they are the specialties of panel members. Tom Trabasso in comprehension, Linnea Ehri in phonics, me for fluency. I fought for my topic as did the others. The outcome could not have been otherwise. That does not compromise the report. It simply demonstrates its limits.
>
> (Samuels 2006)

In 1983, the National Institute of Education commissioned the National Academy of Education to convene a panel to survey the research on reading in order to make recommendations that would promote the United States to become a nation of readers (Richard Anderson, Isabel Beck, Jere Brophy, Jeanne Chall, Robert Glaser, Lenore Ringler, David Rumelhart, Dorothy Strickland and Sue Talbot). In *Becoming a Nation of Readers*, phonics was addressed in a chapter entitled 'Emerging Literacy' that included a range of topics: parental involvement, oral language development, writing, comprehension and materials. The authors discuss research findings and conclude that 'phonics instruction improves children's ability to identify words' (p. 57). They contextualize that statement by referring to the 'natural relationship between word identification and comprehension' and make recommendations for revision of early textbooks to take advantage of that relationship. They return to the topic in the Recommendations sections at the end of the report: 'Phonics instruction should be kept simple and it should be completed by the end of the second grade for most children' (p. 118).

Senator Ed Zorinsky proposed that the Department of Education compile a list of commercial phonics programmes that met the standards of the Commission on Reading in order to inform public schools:

> Mr President, this amendment has been cleared on both sides. It simply follows up on last year's report of the Commission on Reading, Becoming a Nation of Readers ... It is recommended that well designed phonics instruction be used through the second grade, but it did not indicate specifically which beginning reading programs provide such instruction.
>
> (Zorinsky 1986: 1)

The Department packaged Zorinsky's request in its call for proposals for a National Centre for the Study of Reading. P. David Pearson was candid in his acknowledgement that the Centre's funding was contingent on subcontracting a report on phonics instruction: 'We could not ignore this issue' (Pearson 1990: ix). Marilyn Adams's *Beginning to Read* (1990) is that report. Adams provided an encyclopedic treatment of phonics, its place in reading and its teaching. 'In summary, deep and thorough knowledge of letters, spelling patterns, and words, and of the phonological translations of all three, are of inescapable importance to both skillful reading and its acquisition' (p. 426). The problem, she found, was that most of the programmes to teach phonics were 'a waste of time'.

Her report is scholarly, highly technical and lengthy, and passed through an Office of Educational Research and Improvement advisory panel (Ira Aaron, Jeanne Chall, Bernice Cullinan, Linnea Ehri, Philip Gough, Dorothry Strickland and Robert Ruddell). Cullinan and Strickland wrote an afterword for the report to place phonics in its proper context. Before it was released, the Centre for the Study of Reading produced an executive summary to help school personnel glean the expected message from her exhaustive review. According to all reviewers, the summary reduced Adams's argument considerably, promoting explicit and direct instruction in phonics more stridently. Even Adams accepted that this summary simplified her message: 'I guess I agree that it is more firmly centered on the knowledge and processes directly supporting word recognition than the book' (Adams 1991: 390).

In 1995, the Office of Special Education Programs, the Office of Educational Research and Improvement and the National Institute on Child Health and Human Development contracted the National Research Council to convene a committee of experts 'to conduct a study of the effectiveness of interventions for young children who are at risk of having problems learning to read' (Snow 1998: 32). The committee included Catherine Snow (who with colleagues wrote the final report), Marilyn Adams, Barbara Foorman, Edward Kameenui, William Labov, Charles Perfetti, Sally Shaywitz, Keith Stanovich, Elizabeth Sulzby and others. Only one member taught in public schools. According to the report, the committee worked for a consensus model in which definitions of reading and research were reconciled through discussion among members before surveys of existing research were conducted. In this way, the report carries the authority of the committee, the National Research Council and the government agencies. Although the committee was charged to address students at risk, they state, 'our recommendations extend to all children' (p. 32).

Preventing Reading Difficulties in Young Children reiterates the importance of the role of phonics in learning to read. It couples this conclusion with a stronger statement about oral language and phonological knowledge. The committee is more confident in its recommendations for direct instruction than either *Becoming a Nation of Readers* or *Beginning to Read*, perhaps echoing Chall's call for explicit code emphasis for all students. Making an inference from research on expert readers, the committee warns teachers that effective readers do not use context when they read – rather they employ orthographic and phonic knowledge to work through troubling spots in a text. The report does not recommend any specific early reading programme. Rather it suggests that phonics instruction must be accompanied by attention to meaning and a lively oral classroom culture.

Before the *Preventing Reading Difficulties* report was published, Congress directed the head of the National Institute for Child Health and Development and the Secretary of Education to convene a National Reading Panel to review and assess the research on teaching reading with direct implications for classroom practice. The Congressional charge to the Panel set empirical evidence as the criterion for judging the value of reading research related to teaching. Panel members interpreted that criterion, establishing experimentation as the valued form of research. Panel members included Linnea Ehri, Michael Kamil, S. J. Samuels, Timothy Shanahan, Sally Shaywitz, Thomas Trabasso, Johanna Williams and Dale Willows, with one school administrator, Joanne Yatvin. The panel distinguished its work from the *Presenting Reading Difficulties* committee activities by including only experimental studies with sufficient statistical power to be included in the meta-analyses for each of the five categories: Alphabetics, Comprehension, Fluency, Teacher Education and Technology. The panel's choice to include only experimental findings significantly reduced the pool of possible studies on reading and teaching that could be included in their analyses, enabling the statistics to do the work of the other committees. That is, the statistical method, and not the panel members, seems to have determined the conclusions listed in the report.

The National Reading Panel concluded that direct instruction in alphabetics (phonological awareness and phonics), fluency, vocabulary and comprehension were necessary for successful reading achievement. Because of lack of appropriate experimental studies, the panel's recommendations about teacher education and technology were labelled speculative. The Bush administration accepted the report as the justification for the Reading First Initiative within the No Child Left Behind iteration of the Elementary and Secondary Education Act in 2002, which required that each state receiving federal funds for schooling would develop world-class academic standards, test annually each student from the third to the eighth grade and then once in high school on reading (and other subjects), and demonstrate that all students were making adequate yearly progress toward the goal of 100 per cent proficiency by 2014. In order to qualify for funding, states would ensure that all schools were implementing scientific reading instruction based on the National Reading Panel Report with sufficient fidelity in order to reduce the within-method variation among teachers.

The end of history?

In *An Elusive Science: The Troubling History of Educational Research*, Ellen Condliffe Lagemann describes the study of education as a continuing process of specialization in which expertise and authority become defined more narrowly. The study of reading and reading instruction demonstrates this point. Consider the memberships of the committees that set the definitions of both across the twentieth century. Huey attempted to rally psychologists to employ science in order to rationalize reading instruction because teachers and administrators had not accomplished the work. Composed of school administrators and professors of pedagogy, the Committee on the Economy of Time in Education worked inductively to survey the schools in order to develop a scientific management of reading instruction. For the First Grade Studies, professors of education used formal experiments in classrooms across the country in order to determine what worked for reading instruction. The federal reports on reading accelerated the process of specialization, squeezing out the professors of education and replacing them with psychologists. The National Academy of Education's Commission on Reading included four psychologists among its nine members. Psychologist Marilyn Adams worked with an advisory panel with four psychologists. The *Preventing Reading Difficulties* panel members were primarily psychologists and linguists, and the members of the National Reading Panel were nearly all psychologists as well.

As S. J. Samuels concluded in his remarks quoted above, the backgrounds of the committee members who defined reading and reading instruction for a century do not necessarily compromise their reports. They do, however, speak directly to the reports' limitations. As the backgrounds became more consistent across members, consensus was easier to reach; however, it also became easier to exclude diverse definitions, descriptions and values from consideration. At the beginning of the century, Huey sought to exclude teachers' knowledge, historical trends, or publishers' interests. The Committee on the Economy of Time acted to eliminate the craft of teaching. The First

Grade Studies and Chall's *The Great Debate* assumed that child-centred approaches and research had little to offer a definition of reading and reading instruction. The federal reports continued this process until the National Reading Panel excluded all possibilities that history, sociology, anthropology, feminism, politics, race theory, philosophy or literary theory could offer anything of value about reading or reading instruction. Like Pluto in the solar system after the IAU vote, the meaning of this considerable body of work on reading has been changed fundamentally by the panel's decision. And this final (?) report (seven years since its publication) is expected to end the history of reading education.

Reading education in the United States has a parallel here as well. Teachers and schools did not greet the National Reading Panel report as if the one best system had been discovered. School personnel did not rush to remake their reading programmes after the images drawn by the report. And this pattern has been consistent during the last century. If this were not true, Huey's challenge would have been sufficient to change American reading education for the century. But that has not been the case. Teachers and administrators have clung to traditions for some reason, claiming with some justification that their work has been successful.

Consider the *2003 Progress in International Reading Literacy* report. The United States ranked third statistically when reading test scores were compared for 9- and 10-year-old students among 35 nations. It should be noted that these data were collected before NCLB, when the National Reading Panel implied that American teachers did not know how to teach reading. When the report's test scores were disaggregated by income and race, however, the uneven distribution of success in American reading education became apparent. White, non-poor, students scored 24 points above the leading nation, Sweden, while the scores of racial minorities fell among the lowest nations. Whether these biases affirm or create inequalities across social life depends on the political orientation of the interpreter.

Frustrated with the reluctance of school personnel to reform reading education, the Bush administration chose to put the force of the federal government behind the scientific authority of the National Reading Panel, inscribing it as the foundation of the Reading First Initiative within the NCLB law. Reading First required all states to

- develop high standards for reading education;
- test annually between third and eighth grade and once during high school;
- submit such plans and tests for federal approval to ensure that

it followed the evidence-based direction of the National Panel's report.

Let's be clear here. The National Reading Panel's recommendations had to be forced upon schools because its authority could not win in the market of ideas. According to the recent Department of Education Inspector General's report, federal pressure to conform has been considerable. The Inspector General concluded that Reading First leadership selected biased members for review panels of state proposals, which advocated scripted direct instruction in alphabetics through a limited set of commercial programmes. Furthermore, the report found that panel members benefited financially from these forced adoptions. Moreover, the deception appeared to be intentional. Reading First Director Chris Doherty wrote to another official: 'They are trying to crash our party and we need to beat the [expletive deleted] out of them in front of all the other would be party crashers who are standing on the front lawn waiting to see how we welcome these dirtbags' (p. 24).

Perhaps such Machiavellian means could be justified if NCLB and Reading First was 'working' toward its lofty goal to close the gaps between the white and minority and middle- and low-income students. According to the most recent National Assessment of Educational Progress (NAEP) data, however, NCLB is not improving scores in general nor closing the achievement gap, despite five years of phonics first and fast. President Bush's declaration that NCLB is working appears to be based on the modest optimism of the Education Trust report, *Primary Progress, Secondary Challenge* (Hall and Kennedy 2006), which listed modest gains in state reading test scores for elementary school students and little improvement for middle and secondary schools. However, President Bush could not have attended to the Education Trust's concern for the discrepancies between state and national reading test scores. For example, 83 per cent of students reached proficiency on the state test in Alabama 82 per cent in New Jersey and 81 per cent in Oregon. The NAEP proficiency rates were 22 per cent, 37 per cent and 29 per cent respectively. It's clear that phonics-centred instruction is not a natural law, but rather the result of rhetorical struggles between groups with unequal power.

In *Tracking Achievement Gaps and Assessing the Impact of NCLB on the Gaps*, the Civil Rights Project at Harvard University (CRP) argues that the Ed Trust conclusions of early success 'rest on misleading interpretations of flawed data' (Lee 2006: 7) – attending only to the raw numbers who reach proficiency and the gaps between races and income levels and jumping to ideological conclusions based on the organization's support for test-driven changes. CRP emphasizes the national data because the states have a vested interest in showing quick gains in order to qualify for more federal funding. The report's conclusions are direct and devastating to any claims that NCLB and Reading First are working:

1   NCLB has not had a significant general impact on reading achievement across the nation or states. At the current rate of growth only 24 to 34 per cent of American students will reach the required proficiency in 2014 as required by law.
2   NCLB is not closing the racial gaps, although slightly more minority students are reading proficienctly. Only 24 per cent of minorities will reach proficiency by 2014 at the current rate.
3   NCLB has not succeeded in the first generation states (e.g. Florida, North Carolina, and Texas) where NCLB type reforms started before 2002. More time with Reading First conditions does not promise greater success.
4   NCLB state data are misleading, and particularly so for poor and minority students. For white students, state test proficiency rates overstate success at a 2 to 1 ratio of false positives on NAEP. For Black students, the false positives are 4 to 1 between state and national proficiency in reading.

In his introduction to the CRP report, Gary Orfield concluded that 'policy makers must be ready to critically examine why so little has been accomplished, why officials are making misleading and inaccurate claims, and what can be done to use the invaluable data and focus created by the NCLB to begin to actually accelerate progress toward the objectives' (p. 8). By President Bush's criterion, measurement, NCLB has failed. Clearly, forcing teachers to employ direct instruction scripted lessons in alphabetics does not accomplish the goals of enhancing reading achievement in general or overcoming America's historical biases related to class or race to narrow achievement gaps. The National Reading Panel's decision to exclude all research except experimental and correlation studies from their report has not served American schools, teachers and students well. Perhaps Americans should rethink the century of specialization within the reading education field in order to invite new members into the groups who vote to determine the nature of reading and teaching. This group might look back to another pioneer of American psychology, William James, who wrote:

You make a great, a very great mistake, if you think that psychology, being the science of mind's laws, is something from which you can deduce definite programmes and schemes and methods of instruction for immediate schoolroom use. Psychology is a science, and teaching is an art, and sciences never generate arts directly out of themselves.

(James 1901: 31)

Certainly, phonics will appear somewhere in the new definition of reading and within the curriculum as well. Phonics is important, but it is not the centre of the reading instruction solar system.

References

Adams, M. (1991) Response to my critics, *Reading Teacher*, 44: 390.

Adams, M. (1990) *Beginning to Read: Thinking and Learning about Print.* Cambridge, MA: MIT Press.

Anderson, R., Beck, I., Brophy, J., Chall, J., Glaser, R., Ringler, L., Rumelhart, D., Strickland, D. and Talbot, S. (1985) *Becoming a Nation of Readers: The Report of the Commission on Reading.* Washington, DC: NIE.

Austin, M. and Morrison, C. (1963) *The First R.* New York: Wiley.

Bagley, W. (1920) *New Materials for Instruction. 19th Yearbook of the National Society for the Study of Education.* Bloomington, IL: Public School Press.

Barton, A. and Wilder, D. (1964) Research and practice in the teaching of reading, in M. Miles, (ed.) *Innovations in Education.* New York: Teachers College Press.

Bond, G. and Dykstra, R. (1967) The Cooperative Research Program in first grade reading instruction, *Reading Research Quarterly*, 2: 5–142.

Bush, G. W. (2006) Speech in Glen Burnie Elementary School, Maryland, 9 January.

Chall, J. (1967) *Learning to Reading: The Great Debate.* New York: McGraw Hill.

Chall, J. (1999). Some thoughts on reading research: revisiting the First Grade Studies, *Reading Research Quarterly*, 34: 8–10.

Department of Education Inspector General's Report (2006) *The Reading First Program's Grant Application Process*, September. Washington, DC: US Printing Office.

Fukuyama, F. (1992) *The End of History and the Last Man.* New York: Free Press.

Gray, W. S. (1919) Principles in the method of teaching reading as derived from scientific investigation, in E. Horn (ed.) *Fourth Report on the Committee for the Economy of Time in Education.* Bloomington, IL: Public School.

Hall, D. and Kennedy, S. (2006) *Primary Progress, Secondary Challenge: A*

State by State Look at Student Achievement Patterns. Washington, DC: Education Trust.

Huey, E.B. ([1908] 1968) *The Psychology and Pedagogy of Reading.* Cambridge, MA: MIT.

James, W. (1901) *Talks to Teachers on Psychology.* New York: Holt.

Lagemann, E.C. (2000) *An Elusive Science: The Troubling History of Education Research.* Chicago, IL: University of Chicago Press.

Lee, J. (2006) *Tracking Achievement Gaps and Assessing the Impact of NCLB on the Gaps.* Cambridge, MA: Civil Rights Project, Harvard University.

National Reading Panel (2000) *Teaching Children to Read.* Washington, DC: NIH Publications.

Orfield, G. (2006) Introduction, in J. Lee (ed.) *Tracking Achievement Gaps and Assessing the Impact of NCLB on the Gaps.* Cambridge, MA: Civil Rights Project, Harvard University.

Pearson, P. D. (1990) Introduction, in M. Adams, *Beginning to Read.* Cambridge, MA: MIT.

Progress in International Reading Literacy (2003) nces.ed.gov/pubs 2003/2003073.pdf.

Rugg, H. (1941) *That Man May Understand.* New York: Harper.

Samuels, S. J. (2006) Comments made during Hall of Fame Speech About No Child Left Behind, International Reading Association Convention, 3 May, Chicago.

Shannon, P. (2007) *Reading Against Democracy: The Broken Promises of Reading Instruction.* Portsmouth, NH: Heinemann.

Smith, N. B. (1965) *American Reading Instruction.* Newark, DE: International Reading Association.

Snow, C., Burns, S. and Griffin, P. (1998) *Preventing Reading Difficulties in Young Children.* Washington, DC: National Academy Press.

Zorinsky, E. (1986) Amendment to 1986 Human Services Reauthorization Act, *Congressional Record 132*, 90: 1.

5 Teachers' voices: talking about children and learning to read

Andrew Lambirth

In 1991 the Centre for Language (now 'Literacy') in Primary Education published their influential *The Reading Book* (Barrs and Thomas 1991). It was this publication that assisted me, as a teacher in a Southwark school in London at the time, to understand how children learn to read and it has since been used by countless of my own students in shaping their practice in classrooms all around the country. Much of the power of the book comes from the strong links with theory that Myra Barrs and Anne Thomas make, but also from the inclusion of the 'voices' of experienced teachers from classrooms around London. The teachers in *The Reading Book* discuss their own practice and how they have observed their understanding of reading change. For example, one teacher relates how a school she worked in as a novice teacher insisted she use a 'phonics based scheme' (p. 38) called *Royal Road Readers*. She comments, 'Well I thought – anybody could teach reading like this – I mean, you haven't got to be a teacher. I thought there must be more to it than this; there's something radically wrong here' (p. 38). Issues concerning professional autonomy, 'teacher-safe' reading schemes and providing more choice and richer resources for teaching reading were alive 16 years ago in the same way that they are pertinent today. In this present chapter, drawing on the legacy of *The Reading Book*, nursery and primary school professionals from around Kent in England discuss their conception of teaching reading and reflect on the changes they have witnessed over the last 15 years. Like Barrs and Thomas (1991), we too 'hope to be in a better position to define how teachers teach, and what they know' (p. 37).

The teachers in this chapter were informally interviewed by me and Kathy Goouch. They all teach in Kent. Janette and Matthew both practice as teachers in nursery schools. Helen teaches in a Year 2 classroom and Ruth and Roger are Key Stage 2 teachers. At the time of the interviews the Rose Review (Rose 2006) had just been published and the teaching of synthetic phonics, as a 'principal strategy' for early reading, was at the forefront of all our minds.

Our conversation began with a discussion of the teachers' conceptions of what reading is. It moved on to issues to do with reading and its relevance to children. There was a discussion on the pressures put upon teachers and children to reach national standards and this led on to how teaching methods need to be linked to knowledge of child development.

Conceptions of reading

Andrew: Let's talk about reading.

Matthew: I would like to see that children go and pick up books by themselves. Enjoy them, and want to read – that they do different types of reading too. Not just reading fiction but, you know, reading whatever – instructions, non-fiction and so on. I want them to look forward to reading and it is something in their lives that they feel passionate about and want to do.

Ruth: It is really, for me, representation of ideas and meaning kind of locked in a code and once you know how to crack the code then it opens the door to understanding not just printed words, but also ideas and concepts that go beyond.

At this point slight differences of opinions became apparent concerning the nature of reading and the importance of learning how to 'crack a code'. Ruth's view here appears to mirror the notion of reading articulated in the English government's 'Simple View of Reading' introduced in the Rose Review (Rose 2006). This document asks teachers to conceive of learning to read as a linear process that moves from 'learning to read' on to 'reading to learn'. For the government, but not necessarily Ruth, this entails children being given the skills to decode print from grapheme into phoneme by means of synthetic phonics teaching. This appears not to correspond to Matthew's experience of working with very young children in the Foundation Stage in an English nursery school. The notion of learning to read as a linear process and involving a hierarchical system of skills that need to be learned systematically is challenged by Matthew's experiences in his classroom.

Matthew: I don't think you need to crack any codes. My children don't need to crack any codes to read. They can listen to me read a book many times, they can listen to mum and dad read a book many times, they can memorize it and they can sit there and read the book telling a story word perfectly. For me they are reading. Even very young children will read to each other. There is reading for yourself but there is also reading to share something with a friend or whoever, the children can even memorize a book and can sit with a friend and say 'I'm going to read this to you' and off they go and read the book to their friend. This is reading to me too.

Ruth: The first step is really knowing what the point of the words/pictures and everything that is contained in the text is, if we are talking about books specifically. You have to understand the purpose of what's going on. Then you have got to understand the conventions, that you start from the left and work to the right and that it is really about trying to tune into that language, print, which cracking the code and working out what these letters actually mean is part of.

Both teachers agree that children need to understand what reading can offer them. Ruth states that 'then you have got to understand the conventions ...'. Her use of 'then' supports the view that the process of learning to read requires children to understand the relevance of reading in the first instance before 'then' being taught the conventions and technicalities involved in 'cracking a code'. Children making meaning from the texts, for both teachers, is the initial priority for those given the opportunity and responsibility of introducing written words to young children. Yet, the sequence of events that leads children to be able to read independently is what seems to be disputed. The nature of what a child needs to experience in order to read is unresolved at this point in the conversation.

Janette, the other nursery school teacher, comments on the cracking codes and making meaning subject and Helen expands on classroom practices in Key Stage 1. Helen believes that the teacher can introduce a culture and community of readers into the classroom and thus facilitate the construction of an environment that encourages all kinds of reading behaviours.

Janette: To a certain extent it's about decoding print but it's only in terms of being able to make meaning. It's about communicating with somebody who isn't there.

Helen: The first thing I would do is ensure that reading to the children is a regular part of the school day. Reading to the children first of all, and also that they have time to share books with others and read on their own, especially the older children. If they want to, they can choose to be quite quiet readers. What I have seen of the older children is that they like to be in their own world with their own book. Whereas the younger children prefer to share books. The emphasis you give to reading in your classroom, the value you give to it through signs, pictures and displays would encourage them to realize it is important and make them want to do it. If you are excited about books the children will be too. I can remember buying books and taking them in on a Monday and saying, 'I bought this at the weekend' and being really excited about it. The way you are with books rubs off on the children. If you feel like that, they want to read it as well.

Roger: It is more that they experience it than I teach it. I suppose the teaching side of it, as may be imagined by some, doesn't occur very much. You wouldn't walk in and think, 'Ahhh he is teaching them how to read.' The children experience learning to read. So, for example, we use the interactive whiteboard. The picture book texts are always up on there, so they experience reading as a whole class, which they can then see, and respond to. They also sit in small groups and discuss books with me or by themselves.

It is getting them to think about the words in their own heads and to relate to them, using those words and seeing them on the page. They can use them instead of just looking at the words on a page and saying, 'Right, what is that, what is that, what is that?'

Reading and the world

The notion of encouraging young children to find joy, relevance and use for reading comes out very clearly in the comments from the two nursery teachers Janette and Matthew. I found it interesting listening to them talk about 'weaving literacy' into the children's own interests and world. It reminded me of Paulo Freire's writing on teaching literacy to adults and the importance of 'relevance' to the learners' worlds. Freire and Macedo write:

> Reading the word and learning how to write the word so you can later read it are preceded by learning how to write the world, that is, having the experience of changing the world and touching the world.
>
> (Freire and Macedo 1987: 49)

For Matthew and Janette, literacy and learning to read needs to be woven into the very fabric of the children's interactions with their world as it is presented in the classroom. The children are progressively provided with more tools into situations in which it becomes 'inconvenient' not to utilize them.

Kathy: If somebody came into your classroom and asked you about the teaching of reading and what was going on, what would you say?

Janette: We do similar things to what Matthew was saying really as we are trying to work with the individual children's interests and needs. We try and weave literacy into their own interests and promote books and reading through that really, as well as doing a certain amount of explicit teaching during story times and using a lot of story prompts, story sacks and things like that as well. But we tend to weave it in through children's interests so, for example, we have a little girl who has a big interest in snails so we have made sure that we have woven both fiction and non-fiction texts into that, finding information out on the computer to develop that for her. But for us we try and make reading and writing go together; you are writing for someone else to read so they are linked. I don't think you can treat them separately. We pair them up most of the time; we talk about the fact that someone has written the texts they read.

> For us, teaching reading is more incidental. I don't explicitly plan for it; it doesn't appear in my written plan – it just becomes part of the routine that we do, when we are sharing books with a bigger group and so it's not set down as a programme, step one, step two. It's not hierarchical, it's more part of strategies that we would use as we share books with children; we wouldn't do the same things all the time.

Matthew: I do a lot of work with rhyming, it is a big thing. Some of it is planned but a lot of it is, as you say, some of the best things you do are when it's not planned, if a child comes up and says 'My name rhymes with whatever!' Then you go with that. Yes, lots of rhymes. They find it really hilarious when they realize that they can rhyme their name, it's usually a rude thing! They are quite special.

Janette: I think you contrive with literacy and reading to put the child in that situation, don't you, so it becomes inconvenient that they don't know and that they need to know how to use the written word. Which is why I can't balance that with what they call a 'systematic' teaching approach, because that doesn't fit with my beliefs about how young children learn best, which is that they learn when it's inconvenient not to.

Children learn when 'it's inconvenient not to'. This is an interesting point and reveals much about Janette's practice. She has concerns over government documentation (DfES 2006) that champions 'systematic' teaching of synthetic phonics and which is described in the Rose Review (Rose 2006). Using Friere and Macedo's (1987) conceptualization of literacy teaching, Matthew and Janette are allowing the children to use *their* 'world' and *their* 'words' as a tool to understand and control their world. The word is not given to them; they are shown how to utilize the written words they need within the culture that surrounds them.

> Literacy and education in general are cultural expressions. You cannot conduct literacy work outside the world of the culture because education itself is a dimension of culture. Education is an act of knowledge (knowledge here is not to be restricted to a specific object only) on the part of the very subject who knows.
>
> (Freire and Macedo 1987: 51–2)

The children in the classrooms described by Matthew and Janette thrive on using the resources 'to hand' (Kress 1997) (including the written word) to make sense of their world. Using a Bernstein (2003) conceptual framework (see Chapter 7) to understand the pedagogy employed by Janette and Mathew, their teaching has weak hierarchical, sequencing and criterial rules and could be described as a more invisible pedagogy. It is a pedagogy which is more commonly associated with early years practice.

Pressures on teachers

All the teachers were keen to address issues around professional autonomy and the pressures on practice from government agencies and commercial companies peddling schemes. Matthew is the first to begin the discussion.

Matthew: There is pressure that children should be at a certain stage at a certain age at a certain time; for me that just isn't realistic. This is the pressure that we have and it is ridiculous pressure as children will get there with good teaching. I don't think we should be expecting them, as a nation, to all get there by the end of Year 2 or by the end of Year 1 and if some children need more time then why shouldn't they have it? The other thing that annoys me is the ELS (Extra Literacy Support) programmes, that children have got until the Autumn term or the Spring term of Reception and are being told that they are not reading fast enough or that they haven't made enough progress already and they have only been in Reception for two terms and already it is not enough.

Kathy: How old are they?

Matthew: Some of them are not even 5 and that is usually the reason why!

Helen: There are pressures and I think assessment and tracking, trying to follow children's progress through school, which we are doing more of now, means that the impact is there at every stage and doesn't go away. When you are trying to differentiate for children with very different needs it's very hard to cater for every single individual need, so you do tend to group. Or what you might get in lots of schools is that this week we are looking at these letter sounds when half the class can write that letter, can say it and every activity might be based around those letters. What then is that achieving?

Janette: That is more likely to be happening in settings where staff might have little or no training in literacy. In settings in which staff have more training in subject type knowledge and child developmental care this would not be allowed to happen. But I would see very easily the culture coming back and interpretations of new government guidance leading to a slipping back into formal ways of teaching because you think that this is the way that is required.

Roger: From my understanding there is no research that puts systematic synthetic phonics teaching above other ways of reading; it hasn't been proven that this is the way to go. UKLA sent in their response to the Rose Review; it was saying that research doesn't show that there is a difference between the two – analytic and synthetic phonics methods. Again, it comes back to teaching individuals; we aren't teaching groups of robots who learn in one way. It sounds like something that you 'do' to a child rather than the other way around.

Helen: Another thing as well, all the pressures you get from publishers, the types of books that are coming out and courses that are pushed in schools over and over again. 'These are the resources you must have.' Teachers do feel pressure from that and want to buy those things that 'will' save their children from failure. Pressure is coming in that way as well. They are hearing about these methods, when they may not know the background behind them, have done no research but take them on board because they think 'This is what I must do'. There are whole groups of teachers from a range of age phases who tend to adopt every single initiative, scheme and document because they are frightened to let go of them. This material becomes like a safety blanket now because I think they have lost their values, they have had them taken away. I can see why too and I understand; but as professionals we must approach this material with a critical eye.

Ruth: When you are in your classroom it takes a bit of nerve
to say 'No, sorry, I'm trusting my instincts, what I feel
is the right thing to do'. Trust your experience and
your own knowledge of the children and your
professional judgement.

To understand the pressures described by these teachers it is
interesting to read the thoughts of scholars and practitioners in other
English-speaking countries – particularly the United States of America. In
relation to pressures on teachers of reading, US scholars (Shannon 2001;
Dudley-Marling and Murphy 2001) have described how business
principles of efficiency have been imported into the teaching of reading
in the US:

> According to this logic in order to reduce the risk to capital and
> to maximize profits, all aspects of business must become
> predictable ... capitalist logic promises that if all of society
> could be organized in a similar fashion, then society would run
> like a business, creating the best conditions for production,
> technological advance and accumulation. The allure of this
> promise drives the efforts to rationalize more and more aspects
> of public and private life.
>
> (Shannon 2001: 2–3).

For Shannon, scripted lessons, provided by commercial companies,
coupled with high-stakes testing, come directly from the logic of
production. Pedagogy becomes fixed and synchronized and test scores
define a teacher's or child's success and failure. Individuals begin to
forget how teaching and learning is a human process and both teacher
and learner begin to become alienated from the process itself.
Conceptualizing policy for the teaching of reading thus, and applying
it to what the teachers are saying in this chapter, one can detect a strong
resonance. Roger states his doubts about what the Rose Review (Rose
2006) contends about the most effective methods of teaching young
children to read. It could be argued that the intention of the review was
to provide the 'rationalization' for a single method of teaching young
children to read – synthetic phonics. Standardization is made possible,
'production' can now commence. Furthermore, Helen's tale of teachers
blindly utilizing scripted lessons from commercial companies could
suggest that the individuals Helen describes no longer trust their own
human and professional judgements about the children in their classes.
They follow the standardized, rationalized documentation given to them
as a way to increase the chance of higher test scores. According to

Shannon's hypothesis, the teachers that Helen describes have become alienated from understanding their own unique human role as teachers. Furthermore, the children themselves begin to conceptualize reading in terms of their own efficiency as readers, measured by test scores.

Matthew's exasperation at the expectations of children meeting targets of achievement – an educational 'production line' – arguably demonstrates a rationality-driven efficiency drive comparable to any factory productivity score. As Ruth contends, trusting one's experience takes 'nerve'; as looked at from Shannon's (2001) perspective, any attempt by teachers to compose curriculum and begin to improvise practice would be seen as a rejection of rationalization and therefore suspiciously 'political' and subversive.

Child development

The theme of the disjunction between a child's development as a learner and the expectations of a pressurized curriculum and high-stakes testing comes out in the teachers' discussion of how a child develops and learns. They discuss what they see as important strategies for reading that are being ignored in favour of synthetic phonics teaching within official policy documentation. Contextual cues found in illustrations and syntactic cues found and utilized from children's own knowledge of the grammar of spoken language are being sidelined in the Rose Review (Rose 2006) in favour of grapho-phonic cues. All the teachers believe this to be a gross error of judgement by policy makers. The teachers speaking below are convinced that all three cueing systems must be taught from the very beginning of learning about reading.

Andrew: What about the teaching of phonics in your classes?
Matthew: They may have learned a lot of that from home; they may have got that from things that we have talked about as a class, and we talk about the sounds of words. In a nursery it starts a lot earlier than us, but it's quite a long way on to be able to say what is at the beginning of a name, quite a lot has to happen before then. If they are tuning into a beginning of a word they have got to be listening for it.
Janette: Often a lot of children don't pronounce the word chronologically. They haven't actually got it yet. Talking to speech therapists, it's not actually that uncommon for children in nursery not to be able to pronounce certain letters.

Ruth: Is that just a production difficulty?

Janette: I don't know. Imagine if you can't say it, it must be very difficult to hear it and represent it.

Matthew: It's situational.

Janette: In order for you to be able to teach phonics you need to be able to identify the sounds and words that they know.

Matthew: But they also need to be able to listen carefully, and hear and differentiate between different sounds.

Kathy: Do children need to be taught the sounds of letters at this early stage of education?

Janette: Why would a child want to know? Young children are not good at following other people's agendas, especially if there does not appear to be a good reason for doing so other than that our society feels that this is a body of knowledge that children should acquire. But that's not a good enough reason for a 3-year-old or a 4-year-old, is it? So I think there is a problem there to start with; unless we can make it more meaningful you are going to be back to barking at print, which the Rose report tells us is ok.

Matthew: There is no point in trying to get to that stage when you are trying to say letters and sounds. They can be 5, and wherever they are in their development they are not going to be there and if they are not hearing a sound at the beginning of a word, then what's the point in doing what you were talking about, showing them a letter and so on?

Janette: It's all about the use of it, too. We have children in nursery who know the alphabet song and who can join in on the number chant to 20, and their parents are thrilled but they can't use, can't apply any of that information. I wonder if we will be in that position with children who can tell you it's a T and it says TTTTT, in the same way that I have got children who can count to 10 but have no idea how many that is. It's a good skill, 'Well done you', but it's not.

Matthew: It seems to me that the point of a systematic way of teaching reading isn't about fun, it's about speed. That's the only thing that comes across to me. 'We have got to do this as quickly as we possibly can.' It's not about fun or enjoyment of reading, it's about learning a skill, everybody learning as quickly as possible. No matter where we are in our development.

Janette: Somebody said, I think it was Lillian Katz, children can be taught to do all sorts of things at a very young, early age, but that isn't a reason for doing so. It seems that would apply to this; it's about what actually serves children best in the long run isn't it – in life experience? You can teach children to climb up chimneys but that doesn't mean one ought to do it, just because you can teach a child to do it.

Ruth: There is a role for some kind of teaching of phonics; it needs to be done when the child is ready and there is a purpose, in conjunction with the context that reading is a purposeful activity, with lots of stories and word recognition. What puzzled me about the Rose report is that at one point it said that because of the complexities of English the teaching of phonics is essential. I would have thought that this would have been an argument for putting phonics alongside word recognition.

Matthew: It also talks about not encouraging young children to use a range of strategies when they are reading. For beginner readers there are lots of words that they can't work out. Our language is not that phonically regular, so you need to have a range of skills and strategies.

Helen: Going right back to the beginning, thinking about what we just said, and it almost goes full circle in terms of what has been said today about what is reading, it's about communication, about pleasure, about enjoying books and what we have done is gone through all the strategies a child needs to achieve that.

Ruth: I think it is quite unfortunate that this debate has become polarized because the term synthetic phonics has made us all take a deep breath and really it shouldn't. It should be one strategy amongst many.

The teachers talking about reading in this chapter provide a snapshot of the debates, anxieties and conundrums that face teachers on a daily basis. Their professional lives consist of being within the living, breathing exchange and interaction between teacher and learner. They know their children as people, as individuals. These teachers are also carers and they retain a notion that caring is still part of their professionalism. As Barrs and Thomas (1991) contend, 'Teaching reading is a "practical art"; teachers develop their practice by doing it' (p. 36). These teachers are constantly facing challenges to their professionalism and their ability to care for children, which arguably constrains their capacity to develop a practice formed from their own professional activity with the children in their schools. This chapter has contributed to an understanding of 'how teachers teach' in an increasingly politically controlled and contested environment.

References

Barrs, M. and Thomas, A. (1991) *The Reading Book.* London: Centre for Language in Education (CLPE).

Bernstein, B. (2003) 'Social class and pedagogic practice', in *The Structuring of Pedagogic Discourse,* Volume IV: *Class, Codes and Control.* London: Routledge.

DfES (2006) *The Primary National Strategy.* London: DfES.

Dudley-Marling, C. and Murphy, S. (2001) 'Changing the way we think about language', *Language Arts,* 79: 574–8.

Freire, P. and Macedo, D. (1987) *Literacy: Reading the Word and the World.* London: Routledge.

Kress, G. (1997) *Before Writing: Rethinking the Paths to Literacy.* London: Routledge.

Rose, J. (2006) *An Independent Review of the Teaching of Early Reading.* Nottingham: DfES.

Shannon, P. (2001) 'A Marxist reading of reading education', *Cultural Logic,* 4 (1): 2000.

6   To codify pedagogy or enrich learning? A Wengerian perspective on early literacy policy in England

Kathy Hall

Introduction

Those in education, whether student teachers, teachers, teacher educators, researchers, policy makers, parents, school governors, will, to varying degrees, be aware that the teaching of reading in the early years of school continues to be bedevilled by controversy and that in many parts of the English-speaking world governments have urged, indeed insisted, that schools follow increasingly prescriptive pedagogic approaches. I along with many others who have devoted much of their careers to the study and preparation of literacy teachers have written in response to such diktats (Ellis and Lewis 2006; Hall 2006). With reference to current developments in England evidenced in the recommendations of the Rose Review and other official reports (Rose 2006; DfES 2006; DfES 2007), I have argued that the evidence from a variety of sources points to the misguided nature of the particular recommendations about the teaching of phonics. I have also sought to explain the current drive in literacy policy with reference to the discursive and rhetorical role of literacy policy (Hall 2007). In this chapter, however, I take a different angle. Drawing on practice-based learning theory, I explore fundamental ideas about pedagogy and try to explain and demonstrate the inadequacy of adopting a static position. Once the dynamic nature of learning is appreciated, the incompatibility of a strict, unyielding sequence of curriculum content such as we are currently getting in early reading pedagogical recommendations becomes untenable.

The chapter begins by theoretically locating the current preoccupation with the teaching of phonics. It goes on to suggest a richer and more valid way of thinking about pedagogy and the learner and these ways are considered in relation to the policy on early reading in England. The theoretical concepts of reification and participation prove especially useful in understanding the inadequacy of the current pedagogical position and the necessity of a more complex alternative.

Locating Rose in individualistic psychology

One of the problems with the current policy on the teaching of early reading, represented especially in the Rose Review and subsequent official documents on the teaching of reading, is the outmoded learning perspective that it assumes. To explain I will sketch out the assumptions it makes about learners, learning and teaching.

Learning is reduced to individual mental capacity and possession – it is individualistic. This means that, just as success is owned by the individual, so too is failure. Learning can be measured and it is important to establish the different amounts that learners possess. Individual differences matter. There is a strong emphasis on age-dependent patterns of growth and there is an assumption that children will follow a uniform developmental trajectory. A phonics programme, for example, can be set out as a discrete sequential set of skills to be developed which can be explicitly and systematically taught and its effects tested. Phonics programmes in turn may ignore the multiple literacies in which children participate on a daily basis. One kind of literacy, then, is thus privileged in the school. So the phonics programme implemented systematically without much reference to what the learners themselves bring carries whatever wisdom and hidden assumptions that went into its design. The programme organizes action and determines what can be carried out when, where and for what purpose (Cole 1995). Instruction or teaching can be prescribed to foster learning. Teaching is the source of learning – in fact, teaching is necessary for learning to occur. Learning acquired in one context is more or less easy to transfer to another and learning acquired this year can be used in years to come. The acquisition of knowledge and skills can take place in quite a different context from their application – in fact, it is probably better to be removed from day-to-day practical concerns in order for learning to happen. The teacher as transmitter is privileged, the learner as subject is not.

The problem with the conception of pedagogy in the Rose Review is that it reduces teaching to precisely what has to be transmitted into the heads of individual learners. Teaching becomes a set of recipes for delivering a curriculum into the heads of learners. Learners and teachers as subjects with relationships with each other and with the subject world are rendered invisible.

What identities and positions are afforded the teacher in this reified account of how to teach children to read? The teacher is positioned as 'invisible' in the sense that what the teacher thinks and believes is omitted from consideration. There is an attempt to standardize teacher and learner behaviour thereby controlling their goals and values and denying them their expertise. Such a scenario in which the teacher's power to be responsive to learners is so curtailed invites resistance (Day Langhout 2005) since they are bypassed and their power diminished. The silencing of the teacher as pedagogic decision maker arises from the asymmetric power relations. The invisible policy maker makes the rules without ever needing to know the teachers or the learners. The teacher is disciplined and controlled to teach in a particular way while learners are also forced to learn in a particular way. Silencing is cascaded: policy maker silences the teacher and the teacher silences the learner. This level of control seems to be necessary as teachers are perceived to be only a moment away from analytic phonics or whole-word methods or even comprehension.

Their options as to how to respond include self-redefinition and appropriating the new model of being a teacher, resisting the new way through reclaiming counter-narratives based on their own lived experience or some compromise combination of the two that allows them to 'pass' as adhering to the new policy while also remaining faithful to their own professional experiences and views. Whatever position they assume, it will involve shifts in self-definition as professionals vis-à-vis the policy context which will also be influenced, of course, by the stance of the school more generally. Any pedagogic diktats, including prescriptions on phonics, can't easily be copied into school practices because school practices are historically, socially situated practices. This is an area that no doubt merits research, hopefully of an ethnographic kind.

By adopting a mechanistic pedagogy, learners can be classified, labelled, categorized and grouped according to the amount of phonics they appear to possess. Such differences can be made consequential and turned into hierarchies. Teachers will be poised professionally to search for, discover, measure and record phonics progression – on the basis of the research knowledge that is credited with validity and deemed to be absolute (since one teaching method over others has been prescribed). In other words, they will be forced to interpret the interpretations of others (see McDermott 1993; McDermott *et al.* 2006). Teachers are expected to make this knowledge come alive in their pedagogic relations with learners, and certain children will be found to stand out in ways that are consequential because of their phonic knowledge or lack of it. Events and activities will be occasioned so children can be found to be different in the amount of phonic knowledge which they can display and the assumption will be made that their lack is due to their disabilities or incapacities brought on by cultural background, home etc (McDermott *et al.* 2006).

This leads to the conclusion that the language available to talk about phonics (synthetic phonics) becomes a language for talking about and interpreting reading achievement. Phonic knowledge becomes a measure of competence in reading. 'Doing phonics' becomes synonymous with 'doing reading' and for many children the former will prove much more difficult than the latter! Indeed, a cynic might argue that that is the very purpose: the learning of some is fostered at the expense of others. Bureaucratic needs of efficiently sorting individual and life opportunities are manifest in such an assembly-line instructional tradition (Rogoff 1995; Rogoff *et al.* 2003).

From a sociocultural perspective McDermott *et al.* (2006: 16) remind us that 'isolated facts are rarely as important as the preoccupations that elicit them and give them consequence'. And in his ethnography of schooling Jules Henry (1963: 292) observed: 'School metamorphoses the child, giving it the kind of Self the school can manage, and then proceeds to minister to the Self it has made.' We can include in 'the school' the policy maker, the inspector, the parent and so on. The point is that early reading policy has become preoccupied with one way to be a reading teacher and one way to be a reading learner.

There are direct parallels between the pedagogy and the research and learning approach informing the pedagogy. The research evidence that is legitimated by 'scientific' reviews of the teaching of early reading and effectiveness studies (National Reading Panel 2000; Johnston and Watson 2005; Torgerson *et al.* 2006) – research that is increasingly commissioned to fit the bill of 'evidenced-based policy and practice' – tries to adhere to an assumed gold standard represented by the randomized control trial. Such 'rigorous' research generates and codifies a particular kind of knowledge and devalues experience-based knowledge of practitioners. The individualistic account completely ignores the dynamic nature of pedagogy (described next) and therefore it can only at best complement a more participationist account; it can never replace it (Sfard 2006).

The research approach adopted in this line of work is one borrowed from the natural world where the objects of study – individuals – can be treated as static, predictable, and potentially controlled, that is, self-contained biological beings, and where the researcher too is assumed to be able to stand outside the phenomena under investigation. As such the research approach is not just the means of enquiry but is actually the major determinant of the knowledge that it generates and the professional practices it ultimately recommends (Hollway 2001; Biesta 2007), even prescribes. It separates learners and teachers from their contexts, and treats teachers as if they can be separated from the issues under investigation (such as analytic vs synthetic phonics). Criteria for effectiveness are reduced to what is quantifiable. The so-called 'scientific' or 'expert' knowledge that is thus produced is assumed to be objective, neutral and non-ideological. Hidden is the fact that it gets done in the first place because powerful people direct resources to it over alternative studies. Because this kind of research has better access to resources so it has a better chance of imposing its version of truth.

It is beyond the scope of this chapter to develop an argument about what kind of methods are required to produce more valid evidence, except to point out that person, culture and environment/context are inseparable and have to be studied together. While the individualistic psychological approach to research can offer some useful insights, the unit of analysis needs to move beyond the individual to obtain a satisfactory account of pedagogy. Within the realm of pedagogy (see below), where learning is about participation in valued practices and where it is recognized that teacher/teaching and learner/learning can't be examined in isolation, phenomenological and ethnographic methods involving narrative forms of knowledge would be helpful. Latour (1988: 162–63) sums up the different research orientations well:

> There are two ways of displaying powerful explanations ... the first is common to all disciplines: hold the elements of A and deduce – correlate, produce, predict, reorganize, comment or enlighten – as many elements of B as possible. The second is to display the work of extracting elements from B, the work of bringing it to A, the work of making up explanations inside A, the work of acting back on B from A ... In the first, power is reinforced and the represented elements disappear in their representatives. In the second, power is weakened and the initial elements are maintained in full view. The first is reductionist, because holding a single element of A is tantamount to holding all the elements of B. The second I call non-reductionist or 'irreductionist' because it adds the work of reduction to the rest, instead of subtracting the rest once the reduction has been achieved.

A social practice-based, relational pedagogy

An alternative and nuanced way of thinking about pedagogy derives from the work of Jean Lave, Etienne Wenger, Barbara Rogoff, James Wertsch and others, which I can only sketch briefly here. It is fundamentally different to the one outlined above and it is infinitely more complex and in my opinion more challenging to understand which no doubt contributes to its lack of uptake not only by policy makers but also by some researchers of teaching and learning. Practice-based theories deal with the dynamics of everyday life: interactions, improvizations, negotiations, meanings, interpretations, participations and intentions. This pedagogy foregrounds the ownership of meanings and so involves social participation and relations of power. This social practice account does not involve mechanistic transmission; rather it allows for 'the active role of unique agents carrying out unique actions', although these unique agents and actions are mediated by shared cultural tools like language (Hatano and Wertsch 2001: 79). As well as taken-for-granted ways of using language, other cultural tools include common-sense knowledge and beliefs and ways of organizing people (for learning how to read). The environment or 'surround'; i.e. what is there socially, in this sense does part of the thinking and learning. Here learning is conceptualized as an aspect of changing participation in socially situated practices using the tools and artefacts associated with communities of practice. All learning is situated – there is no other kind of learning except situated learning.

In contrast with learning as internalization (above), learning understood as increasing participation in communities of practice concerns the whole person acting in the world. And participation is always based on people negotiating and renegotiating meaning in the world such that understanding and experience are in constant interaction and flux. What is learned according to this version of pedagogy is not a static subject matter but the very process of participating in and developing an ongoing practice. Wenger says 'practice is both road and destination' and 'what we learn with the greatest investment is what enables participation in the communities with which we identify. We function best when the depth of our knowing is steeped in an identity of participation, that is, when we can contribute to shaping the communities that define us as knowers' (Wenger 1998: 60 and 253). The kind of dualisms between, say, mind and body, abstraction and experience, reflection and participation disappear in this way of thinking about learning. This view also recognizes that while opportunities for participating are essential, they are not equally available to all.

What is of concern is the practice – what is the practice and how do learners become imbued with the practice? In relation to reading pedagogy a key question might be: who and where are the embodied exemplars of what 'readers' are becoming? For people become kinds of persons – learning involves becoming more competent in an aspect of participation in social practice. So the kind of person you are becoming shapes what you know. The notion of 'doing' rather than 'knowing' gets to the point of it, e.g. 'doing' phonics (reading!) as opposed to having acquired phonic knowledge. The notion of learning skills or knowledge to be acquired for later application in another context is inadequate. Learning is fundamental and teaching is not an explanation for learning. Teaching is neither necessary nor sufficient for learning to occur (Lave 1996).

In this perspective on pedagogy, teachers and learners are located participants – they have identities, or, put another way, they are already members of various communities of practice that matter to them; they are variously evolving, aspiring, marginalized, peripheral, full members of communities of practice including school communities of practice. Teachers need to know about the 'powerful identity-changing communities of practice' (Lave 1996: 157) of their pupils since these 'define the conditions of their work'. A question for the reading teacher in this perspective becomes: how do I make children participate in reading as part of their collective identity-changing lives?

Rose again: reification and participation

The Rose Review and the programmes, policy documents and materials that are designed to maximize the faithful implementation of its recommendations can all be considered as an attempt to stabilize meaning regarding what reading is in the early years of school as well as an attempt to impose teacher and learner identities. Such artefacts or mediating resources offer identity kits or blueprints for a way to be as learner and teacher. In the remainder of this chapter I will draw heavily on the work of Etienne Wenger (1998) and in particular his notions of *reification* and *participation* to highlight the inadequacy of the current policy on the teaching and learning of early reading. I will argue that the Rose version of teaching reading in the early years only deals with one side of the coin – *reification* – and ignores the equally vital other side, namely *participation*. Participation and reification are extremely useful conceptual tools for understanding the way people appropriate what is available to be learned. While the impetus for this discussion stems directly from the new policy in England about phonics, the argument I am making could be attributed to any attempt to control pedagogic meanings in the way Rose does.

The opportunity to participate, to negotiate meaning is fundamental to learning. *Participation* is one side of the coin. What counts as participation or what members of a community deem relevant and worth attending to, as represented in the objects we create to illustrate practices, is the other side of the coin – Wenger terms this *reification*. He suggests that we project our meanings on to the world and then we act as if these meanings exist in the world as having a reality all of their own.

Reification gives form to experience by producing objects; it turns experience into a thing. According to Wenger it covers a

> wide range of processes that include making, designing, representing, naming, encoding and describing as well as perceiving, interpreting, using, reusing, decoding and recasting ... from entries in a journal to historical records, from poems to encyclopedias, from names to classification systems, from dolmens to space probes, from the Constitution to a signature on a credit card slip, from gourmet recipes to medical procedures, from flashy advertisements to census data, from single concepts to entire theories, from the evening news to national archives, from lesson plans to the compilation of text-books, from private address lists to sophisticated credit-report-ing data bases, from tortuous political speeches to the yellow pages. In all these cases aspects of human experience and practice are congealed into fixed forms and given the status of object.
>
> (Wenger 1998: 60)

Parallels in reading pedagogy are: the policy statement, the 'map' of where to go and how to get there, the lesson plan, the textbook, the phonics materials. Wenger lists all of the following as levers within reification: legislation, policies, expositions, statistics, contracts, plans and designs. The Rose Review and its spin-off products become points of focus around which meaning is negotiated and organized. The reification products are reflections of practices 'frozen into a text' but inevitably incapable of capturing the richness of lived experience. Examples of reification are also symbols, stories, terms, abstractions – all of which are forms that seek to capture experiences and practices (or participation) and pin them down as a fixed form which is used then to guide and change practices (participation). In this way reification shapes our participation. Reification can make up for the limits of participation or action (and vice versa). Our participation changes as a result of reification. Reification changes our experience of the world. Levers of participation, on the other hand, include: personal authority, nepotism, discrimination, charisma, trust, friendship and ambition. Both sets of levers can shape the development of practice.

Reification is not merely object, though, since it must be appropriated at local level to be rendered meaningful. This means that reification products (exemplified by the phonics policy statement, materials and so on) imply participation (exemplified in our case by the actual teachers and learners who will make it happen in practice). Although they are distinct from each other, reification and participation fit around each other. One implies the other; they are relational. This is how Wenger eloquently expresses the relation between them: 'They cannot be transformed into each other, yet they transform each other. The river only carves and the mountain only guides, yet in their interaction, the carving becomes the guiding and the guiding becomes the carving' (Wenger 1998: 71).

But what is the proportion of the relationship in our case? Or what is reified and what is left to participation? Wenger demonstrates that the 'communicative ability of artifacts depends on how the work of negotiating meaning is distributed between reification and participation' and that 'different mixes become differently productive of meaning' (Wenger 1998: 64). He goes on to explain how the balance needs to be right, that when too much reliance is on one at the expense of the other, 'the continuity of meaning' becomes compromised in practice. He says: 'If participation prevails – if most of what matters is left unreified – then there may not be enough material to anchor the specificities of coordination and to uncover diverging assumptions. This is why lawyers want everything in writing' and 'If reification prevails – if everything is reified, but with little opportunity for shared experience and interactive negotiation – then there may not be enough overlap in participation to recover a coordinated, relevant, or generative meaning. This helps explain why putting everything in writing does not seem to solve all our problems' (Wenger 1998: 65). Wenger is highlighting two things. First, that there is the duality, interaction and the interplay between reification and participation; they are not dichotomies or separate categories and it is certainly not a question of reification as 'bad', participation as 'good'. As dualistic they have to be considered in tandem. Second, that the balance between them must be such that one can compensate for the inadequacies of the other.

From the point of view of my focus in this chapter, what is of interest is the nature of the relation or the interplay between reification and participation in the context of the current phonics prescriptions. Specifically can/will the Rose artefacts support the communities of practice for which they are destined? While the policy can be prescribed or recommended to the point of *de facto* prescription, it must still submit to negotiation at the level of participation in communities of practice because the negotiation of meaning is always fluid and the outcomes indeterminate. As Wenger notes, the critical issue is negotiability, not authority. Will teachers be able and willing to make sense of the reification and take ownership over its meaning in the broadest context of extending their pupils' literacy competence or will the reification stifle negotiation of meaning? The lack of engagement with the professional community including teacher educators means that the negotiation of meaning was not part of the current policy and so it is highly likely that teachers at best will struggle to make it their own. Other people, not teachers, have put boundaries around what reading pedagogy is. A Wengerian analysis suggests that when there is such a division between those who produce and those who adopt meaning, as there is in this case, then ownership of meaning is inevitably one sided. He concludes that where such a situation persists it results in 'a mutually reinforcing condition of both marginality and inability to learn' (Wenger 1998: 203). The new meanings of reading pedagogy belong to someone but not to teachers – for some teachers the new meanings may not be there to access, never mind own. Teachers are being asked to assume the meaningfulness of what they do. The 'simple view of reading', with its pedagogic notion of decoding followed by comprehension, together with a very specific (and exclusive) phonic approach to the promotion of decoding, would suggest that what is to be learned is so deeply codified, reified and stylized that any authenticity is removed. Wenger says that 'the impossibility of appropriating alien meanings turns the alien character of meaning back onto the identity of the interpreter. They become meanings of non-participation' (Wenger 1998: 205).

Conclusion

A prescriptive pedagogic stance requiring literal compliance minimizes ownership and teachers may well simply ventriloquate the new discourse, thus masquerading as conforming. Bakhtin used the term ventriloquation to mean that one voice speaks through another voice, or voice type (Wertsch 1991). Undoubtedly some people will and have argued that such alignment to the reification is efficient as it allows teachers to bypass the complex process of negotiating and sharing meaning about reading pedagogy, say at school level. The problem is that this literal dependency on the reification, as Wenger's work illustrates, thwarts the ability to respond to the unforeseen and unpredictable. It stifles opportunistic teaching; it narrows the space for the negotiation of meaning. I am not advocating a rejection of authority and a *laissez-faire* approach in which all teachers have to make up their own minds and reinvent the wheel. What is at issue is the relationship between the planned and the practice, and the ability of teaching to connect with learning. And currently I suggest that early reading policy and early years practice are in gross disproportion.

If teachers are persuaded by the phonics artefacts, if they buy in to the way of being a teacher that is held out in the various phonics documents, such identification by its nature limits their negotiability. Ultimately, however, the question will be the extent of the power of the Rose paraphernalia to evoke meaning and the nature of such meaning making in different spaces. We will need accounts of how the teacher, as complex self, negotiates new meanings around the many uniform representations of phonics practices in current official documents.

References

Biesta, G. (2007) Why 'what works' won't work: evidence-based practice and the democratic deficit in educational research, *Educational Theory* 57 (1): 1–22.

Cole, M. (1995) Sociocultural settings, in J. Westsch (ed.) *Sociocultural Studies of Mind*. New York: Cambridge University Press.

Day Langhout, R. (2005) Acts of resistance: student (in)visibility, *Culture and Psychology* 11 (2): 123–58.

DfES (2006) *Primary Framework for Literacy and Mathematics: Core Position Papers Underpinning the Renewal of Guidance for Teaching Literacy and Mathematics*. London: DfES.

DfES (2007) *How to Choose an Effective Phonics Programme: Core Criteria and Guidance*. London: DfES. Available at http://www.standards.dfes.gov.uk/phonics/programmes/

Hall, K. (2006) How children learn to read and how phonics helps, in M. Lewis and S. Ellis (eds) *Phonics Practice, Research and Policy*. London: Sage Publications.

Hall, K. (2007) Reading policy and policy literacy: a tale of phonics in early reading, in J. Soler and R. Openshaw (eds) *Reading Across International Boundaries*. London: Routledge.

Hatano, G. and Wertsch, J.V. (2001) Sociocultural approaches to cognitive development: the constitutions of culture in mind, *Human Development*, 44: 77–83.

Henry, J. (1963) *Culture against Man*. New York: Vintage Press.

Hollway, W. (2001) The psycho-social subject in 'evidence-based practice', *Journal of Social Work Practice*, 15 (1): 9–22.

Johnston, R. and Watson, J. (2005) *The Effects of Synthetic Phonics Teaching on Reading and Spelling Attainment: A Seven Year Longitudinal Study*. Available at http://www.scotland.gov.uk/Resource/Doc/36496/0023582.pdf.

Latour, B. (1988) The politics of explanation, in S. Woolgar (ed.) *Knowledge and Reflexivity*. London: Sage Publications.

Lave, J. (1996) Teaching, as learning, in practice, *Mind, Culture, and Activity* 3 (3): 149–64.

Lave, J. (nd) *Everyday Life*. Available at http://www.si.umich.edu/ICOS/Presentations/041699, accessed 8 May 2006.

Lave, J. and Wenger, E. (1991) *Situated Learning: Legitimate Peripheral Participation*. Cambridge: Cambridge University Press.

McDermott, R. (1993) The acquisition of a child by a learning difficulty, in S. Chaiklin and J. Lave (eds) *Understanding Practice: Perspectives on Activity and Context*. Cambridge: Cambridge University Press.

McDermott, R., Goldman, S. and Varenne, H. (2006) The cultural work of learning disabilities, *Educational Researcher*, 35(6): 12–17.

National Reading Panel (2000) *Teaching Children to Read: An Evidence-based Assessment of the Scientific Research Literature on Reading and its Implications for Reading Instruction*. Washington, DC: National Institute of Child Health and Human Development.

Rogoff, B. (1995) Observing sociocultural activity on three planes: participatory appropriation, guided participation, and apprenticeship, in J.V. Wertsch, P. del Rio and A. Alvarez (eds) *Sociocultural Studies of Mind*. New York: Cambridge University Press.

Rogoff, B., Paradise, R., Mejia Arauz, R., Correa-Chavaz, M. and Angelillo, C. (2003) First hand learning through intent participation, *Annual Review of Psychology*, 54: 175–203.

Rose, J. (2006) *Independent Review of the Teaching of Early Reading: Final Report*. London: DfES.

Sfard, A. (2006) Telling ideas by the company they keep: a response to the critique by Mary Juzwik, *Educational Researcher* 35 (9): 22–7.

Torgerson, C.J., Brooks, G. and Hall, J. (2006) *A Systematic Review of the Research Literature on the Use of Phonics in the Teaching of Reading and Spelling*, Research Report 711. London: DfES.

Voelklein, C. and Howarth, C. (2005) A review of controversies about social representations theory: a British debate, *Culture and Psychology*, 11 (4): 431–54.

Wenger, E. (1998) *Communities of Practice: Learning, Meaning, and Identity*. New York: Cambridge University Press.

Wertsch, J.V. (1991) *Voices of the Mind: A Sociocultural Approach to Mediated Action.* Hemel Hempstead: Harvester Wheatsheaf.

Wertsch, J. V. (1998) *Mind as Action.* New York: Oxford University Press.

7 Social class and the struggle to learn to read: using Bernstein to understand the politics of the teaching of reading

Andrew Lambirth

> Who, then, are the children who do not fare well in early reading? Some are children with genuine neurological disorders making learning to read quite difficult. But the majority are poor or come from minority groups whose members have faced a history of prejudice and oppression (Snow *et al.* 1998) ... why should being poor or a member of a particular social group have anything whatsoever to do with learning to read in school? Isn't the whole purpose of public schooling to create a level playing field for all children?
>
> Gee (2004: 7)

As acknowledged by the present British government (DfES 2004), economic inequality is often mirrored by inequalities in achievement at school. Furthermore, differences in economic status and consequently differences in social class and power contribute to dissimilarity in the cultural practices – the 'primary discourses' (Gee 2004) – between dominant and subordinated groups in society. In other words, the form of consciousness that has been mediated in informal circumstances and in specific social environments is a powerful determinant of how children will respond in structured cultural school settings (Hasan 2004). Some forms of consciousness, mediated by cultural semiotic tools, are valued more than others. I will argue in this chapter that learning to read is primarily a cultural process (Gee 2004). Bernstein (2003) contended that pedagogic practice is a means by which cultures and specific forms of consciousness are promoted, reproduced and relayed. In so doing, specific cultures are promoted and others ignored or denigrated. By drawing on the later work of Bernstein (1990, 1996, 2003) and linking it to the work of Vygotsky (1978a, 1978b, 1981), I intend to make a connection between Bernstein's conceptualization of pedagogies and the methods for the teaching of reading that are being debated elsewhere in this book. I distinguish between the pedagogy of learning to read and the content of that pedagogy. But, as I shall argue, those who highlight the need to teach specific skills (traditionalists) and those who advocate providing children with 'reading experiences' (whole-language approaches) present pedagogies to carry these transmissions. Using Bernstein's theoretical position, pedagogies of reading can be seen as being permeated by social class assumptions and linked to the values and social reproductive aspirations of those fractions of the middle class from whom they derive. Advocates of one single method of teaching reading promote one form of cultural relay at the expense of others and arguably promote the social reproduction of the inequalities of society that are powered by underachievement in school. Yet, whatever pedagogy is advocated and used by these different fractions of the dominant culture, those who struggle the most with reading will be those to whom Gee refers in the opening quote of this chapter – subordinated groups. By making this argument, my intention is not to construct a wholly negative, deterministic and hopeless perspective (indeed, this would be misleading and unhelpful). I wish instead to generate an understanding of how Bernstein reveals the complex and socioculturally orientated nature of underachievement and how achievement in school and in learning to read can be a major enterprise for some compared to others.

Ultimately, as will be shown, this theoretical position contends that the answers are political rather than residing in the educational environment alone. It demands active engagement in politics and self-awareness of the origins of one's beliefs and principles concerning how children learn to read. In my attempt to understand how there is a struggle to learn to read for many in our society I briefly examine working-class underachievement; I go on to contrast the concept of 'acquiring' and 'learning' knowledge and examine how the cultures within which we learn are formed. The nature of pedagogies of reading is compared, and their cultural and class assumptions exposed. In presenting these positions I wish to show how the inequalities that are endemic in society are transposed onto reading pedagogy.

I begin with a short description of ongoing patterns of under-achievement from working-class children. I then conceptualize the processes of learning using a particular framework and match these notions with two broad pedagogical traditions for the teaching of reading. I will then go on to discuss the phenomenon of social reproduction and Bernstein's conceptualization of pedagogy and how this relates to the two broad traditions of the teaching of reading.

Working-class underachievement

Working-class children do learn to read. However, there is a great deal of evidence that highlights how levels of economic prosperity and social class are the best predictors of success or underachievement in school (Smith *et al.* 1997; Beckett 2000; McCallum and Redhead 2000; Thomas 2000; DfEE 2000; DfES 2004; Hatcher 2006). For example, a recent longitudinal study (Sylva *et al.* 2003) that looked at 3000 children, from entry into pre-school to the end of Key Stage 2, showed that a 5-year-old whose parents earn more than £67,500 will have reading skills six months in advance of those whose parents are jobless.

In the United Kingdom today the richest 10 per cent get nearly 28 per cent of the total income, while the poorest 10 per cent get under 3 per cent (Denny and Elliott 2004; Hatcher 2006). These levels of inequality have increased since the New Labour government came into power. The poorest proportion of society had 7 per cent of the nation's wealth in 1996 and 5 per cent in 2001 (Foot 2003). As a result of this economic inequality and status, the present government acknowledges the impact on educational achievement:

> Those from higher socio-economic groups do significantly better at each stage of our system than those from lower ones – indeed socio-economic group is a stronger predictor of attainment than ability.
>
> (DfES 2004: 20)

Bernstein (2003) argued that in most official educational settings where a visible pedagogy (discussed later in this chapter) is dominant, early learning to read is crucial. The age-related expectations and the fast pace of pedagogy in most schools makes the ability for independent, non-oral, solitary work highly necessary: '... those children who are unable to meet sequencing rules as they apply to reading become more dependent upon the teacher and upon oral forms of discourse' (2003: 205). Age-related educational expectations make the ability to read early crucial. As the government concurs:

> In general, though, those that do well early do even better later on in life, while those that do not perform well fall further

behind; and the chances of breaking out of this cycle of underachievement reduce with age.

(DfES 2004: 21)

The rate at which children learn to read is a major factor in achievement in schools. As I intend to show, reading is primarily a cultural process and children's introduction to particular forms of literacy developed in a specific culture will influence their development as readers and learners in school. By providing this important understanding of patterns of underachievement, I do not want to construct a purely deterministic perspective. Working-class children do learn to read and many succeed in educational settings. Yet, it is clear from a great deal of research that some children will come to school more advantaged than others and better prepared to undertake the sequencing of the pedagogy and the national expectations of achievement. It is important now to begin to create a conceptualization for the processes of learning that will frame the later discussions in this chapter.

'Acquiring' and 'learning' literacy

Gramsci (1971) saw literacy as being both a practice monopolized by the dominant class and culture in order to maintain this dominance and also a means by which individuals obtain self and social empowerment, escaping subordination. For Gramsci, literacy is a terrain of struggle. It belongs to the struggle

> over the orders of knowledge, values, and social practices that must necessarily prevail if the fight for establishing democratic institutions and a democratic society (is) to succeed.
> (Giroux 2005: 147–48)

The pedagogy of literacy, then, is part of a struggle vital to securing which side of the double-edged sword of literacy will prevail. It will be argued that, despite fierce disagreements amongst advocates of contemporary literacy pedagogies, most remain in the domain of middle-class dominant cultures and consciousness and contribute to social reproductive practices that replicate inequality. To understand the debates over the teaching of reading something needs to be said about conceptualizations of gaining knowledge of a literacy and how the most efficient ways of learning are mostly situated within one's own culture.

There is arguably an important distinction to be made between the 'acquisition' and 'learning' (Krashen and Terrell 1983) of knowledge.

Krashen and Terrell maintain that through *acquisition* one gains knowledge subconsciously by the models provided by others and through a process of trial and error. The settings in which one acquires this knowledge are those which are familiar to the acquirer and where there is a meaningful and functional context to what is being acquired. *Learning*, on the other hand, still using Krashen and Terrell's (1983) analysis, is a process through which knowledge is gained through teaching or instruction. In this model, aspects of the knowledge to be learned are broken down, analysed and explained. However, for both the acquisition and learning of knowledge, some form of pedagogy or mediation is required, either official and planned, or unofficial and/or unplanned: 'Much of what we come by in life, after our initial enculturation, involves a mixture of acquisition and learning. However, the balance between the two can be quite different in different cases and different at different stages in the process' (Gee 2001: 3). As Gee (2004) argues, becoming a reader, indeed like most forms of knowledge and skill, happens more readily when the emphasis is on acquisition rather than learning or instruction. In other words, when reading forms part of one's day-to-day life, when those around you model reading and value the activity and it is meaningful, pleasurable and functional, reading becomes an acquisition, and any instruction thereafter acts as an alternative form of conceptualizing the process.

The ferocious arguments between the so-called traditionalists (e.g. Stanovich 1993) and the so-called progressives (e.g. Routman 1996) centre around the advantages or disadvantages of instruction/'learning' that emphasizes skills rather than meaning compared with methods that promote environments conducive to acquisition and emphasize meaning rather than skills. But in order to understand these two positions, more needs to be said about cultures and how they are formed to help understand how one acquires different social and semiotic practices.

Semiotic mediation

To understand how human beings differ in terms of their conceptualization of the world and how they interact with it, Vygotsky (1981) describes how behaviours are developed and consequently how cultures are formed by the mediation of tools.

Vygotsky conceptualized language and other sign systems as being an important tool which mediates human action. In the socio-genesis of the organization of human behaviour, the intervention of a variety of tools was vital. The use of concrete tools, for example, was able to change the very nature of human physical activity and achievement, ultimately

transforming the environment in which humans exist through mediation by these technical tools. Similarly, mental labour was transformed
by the use of mental tools. Mediation by tools in this sphere of human
existence transforms the nature and quality of mental functions and
forms the people we are (Vygotsky 1981).

For Vygotsky, semiotic mediation was mediation by means of the
linguistic sign – a language. He wanted to examine how language
transformed a biological organism into a social person and how the
acquisition of language affected the behaviour of people as they
developed. One might interpret this as how people use words – their
literacy and the literacy events which form part of their day-to-day living
– and how this literacy mediates how they make meaning and ultimately
how they conceptualize the world, constructing their own identity
within that world and culture. This is a 'way with words' that is
'acquired' rather than 'learned'. Borrowing a term from Bernstein, Hasan
(2004) describes this as *invisible semiotic mediation*. This, unlike visible
semiotic mediation, is not pedagogically generated and occurs without
either of the two parties concerned being aware that the process or
content of mediation is occurring. Bernstein (2000) has written that 'All
experiencing carries pedagogic potential but not all experiences are
pedagogically generated' (p. 199). Hasan's (2004) view is that mediation
is different to pedagogy: 'Things get mediated whether or not they are
generated with mediation in mind' (p. 39).

The uses of language around a developing person mediate the
construction of knowledge and, consequently, a person's identity and
culture. There is much contemporary research to support the view (Brice
Heath 1983; Street 1984; Hall 1987; Lankshear 1987; Barton 1994; Taylor
1997; Gee 2004) that literacy is acquired in many forms and is fashioned
by environment. What many scholars fail to show, however, is that these
cultures are not given equal status in society and that some are dominant
and others are subordinated in order to secure the continuation of
particular social and economic inequalities.

Arguably, here resides the source of problems with learning to read
and with general achievement in school. It is here that the subordinated
cultures must achieve in institutions dominated by the powerful ruling
cultures of society whose very objective, according to some sociologists,
is to reproduce the sociocultural power relations manifested in the form
of social class relations (Bourdieu and Passeron 1977). As will be
discussed later in this chapter, certain forms of pedagogy relay and
privilege certain forms of culture (Bernstein 2003) and have social class
assumptions which can be alien to these subordinated cultures. These
pedagogies are value-laden and have been developed within language-
mediated environments that have formed distinct forms of conscious-

ness (Vygotsky 1981). The hypothesis generated from this form of theoretical understanding is that in order to achieve at the same rate as the dominant cultures with which these pedagogies are associated, a conscious, consistent and robust trans-cultural perspective from the teacher, the child, the parents and society as a whole will be necessary. Furthermore, a consistent and high level of financial capital will also be required if the children from subordinated groups are to maintain these levels of achievement equal to dominant social classes – a 'tall order' that begins to explain the levels of underachievement in specific sections of society.

The pedagogies of reading disclose the perspectives of their advocates. The tradition behind each reading pedagogy will now be addressed. I will then go on to conceptualize these methods from Bernstein's theoretical perspective. In doing so, I hope to expose the social class and cultural assumptions that exist within them.

Traditionalists and progressives in the teaching of reading

The traditionalist argument stresses the need for beginner readers, as young as 3 in some circumstances, to be first taught the basic skills of written language, 'especially those that take apart sounds within words, connect sounds to make words, associate sounds and letters and identify sight words' (Coles 2000: x). Those new to reading must gain these skills first in order to apply them rapidly to different texts they may meet. Young children, according to this argument, need to obtain these skills first, as they have limited memory at their disposal and would become confused by the need to apply other strategies or to concentrate upon the meaning (Coles 2000). Therefore, as argued by traditionalists, teachers need to provide these skills through a range of teacher-led activities, including 'chalk and talk' methods, chanting, games initiated and led by the teacher and regular testing. The children's personal access to texts would need to be limited to those which contain only the words the children have been learning. In some models (RRF 2006) only the teacher is sanctioned to read from more linguistically complex and more 'interesting' (RRF 2006: 2) texts to help maintain motivation and increase vocabulary. Homework is likely to be in the form of sets of letters to practise sounding phonemes and how to blend them with others. There may also be a graded reading scheme book with which to practise their newly learned skills. The emphasis can be conceptualized, as was discussed in the early part of this chapter, on 'instruction' or 'learning' as opposed to 'acquisition'.

Traditional approaches assume that literacy consists of discrete skills that need to be taught in isolation from the language contexts from which they derive. The pro-phonics-only Reading Reform Foundation's (2006) response to the new English Primary National Strategy (DfES 2006) quotes the Rose Review of Teaching Early Reading (Rose 2006) as stating that

> Beginners should be taught grapheme–phoneme correspondences from simple to complex and in a clearly defined, incremental sequence ... Children's mastery of the decoding and encoding skills taught up to any given point (grapheme–phoneme correspondences, blending and segmenting) should be frequently assessed and appropriate teaching should be provided for those who need it.
>
> (p. 2)

The pace of learning these skills is also often emphasized. Macnair describes her conversion to traditionalist methods of teaching reading using synthetic phonics after observing pro-phonics teachers in action:

> From these sessions my first impression was that of speed. The pace of the lessons was very slick and well structured. Letters and sounds were introduced with up to four sounds a week, which was much quicker than any approach I had previously experienced.
>
> (Macnair et al. 2006: 46)

Macnair describes how she 'developed a blueprint which I now use with most classes I teach' (Macnair et al. 2006: 46). Her 30- to 40-minute lessons are fast paced, and maintain a set pattern of procedures which are applied to all children, whatever their background experiences. She groups 'the children sitting in front of the chalkboard in rows or in a circle with magnetic boards within reach' (p. 46). The organization of Macnair's lessons can be described as traditional, indeed, arguably, even Victorian in nature. Movement appears to be highly controlled and restricted. The organization, despite some concessions to participation by the children themselves, has an emphasis on transmission models of teaching and learning.

Traditionalists promote 'learning' as opposed to 'acquisition' to gain the knowledge required to become a reader. The environment for this form of pedagogy needs to be formal, with instruction applied at a fast pace and where objectives are set and criteria for success made explicit and regular testing essential.

The so-called progressive movement presents a different pedagogy. The 'whole-language' movement is historically the traditionalists' main adversary (Coles 2000). The emphasis of this pedagogy is to guide early readers to understand the meaning of a given text and to make personal, intellectual connections with that meaning. Importantly, the 'whole-language' movement conceives children's motivation to become readers as being similar to children's motivations to comprehend the oral forms of language:

> Just as their making of and communicating with oral meaning was the over-arching orchestration that promoted their pronunciation of words, use of words to identify multiple objects, strings of words into sentences, syntax, and vocabulary development, and so forth, making of and communicating with written meaning has similar effects.
>
> (Coles 2000: xi)

Advocates (Routman 1996) of the 'whole-language' movement argue their pedagogy will teach the basics but in a meaningful context with a greater emphasis on social relationships and learning communities. There would be more opportunities for independent reading and more freedom over the texts to which the children have access and from which they can choose. Progressive pedagogues will not set specific instructional homework tasks, but will be more likely to produce information leaflets for parents that encourage certain literacy practices in the home (Marsh 2006). For example, bedtime reading and other daily informal contact with children's literature and other written material found within the environment would be encouraged to be utilized.

Organization of 'whole-language' classrooms has more of an emphasis on collaboration and the children's independence from the teacher. Evans (Macnair *et al.* 2006) describes her classroom environment:

> My literacy teaching starts with the classroom environment. There are plenty of attractive books (fiction and non-fiction) and comfortable carpeted areas where we gather to read, as a class, a group or individually.
>
> (p. 51)

Children in Evans's class are enticed into areas away from desks and chalkboards. A liberation of movement within a space for the children is suggested from her comments. The teacher and children are united as readers by Evans's use of 'We gather to read'. Her role as the teacher is constructed as being less visible than in Macnair's classroom. Evans's authority and her hierarchical position are relaxed and her identity as an adult in the classroom is more informal and 'homely'. Yet, as Perkins and Goodwin (Macnair *et al.* 2006) point out, some of this is a friendly facade:

> A language and literacy rich classroom can be deceptive. It may look disorganised and unsystematic but the bedrock which underpins the excitement and activity is well-planned, systematic teaching. Every encounter with print will be planned to allow children to learn about both the nature and the function of written language.
>
> (p. 56)

These comments from broadly 'whole-language' advocates present a more progressive approach but, as Bernstein's work shows, under the surface of much of what is presented as more liberated practice lies a traditionalist stance. Behind what some may perceive as the 'chaos' of a whole-language classroom a very visibly controlled pedagogy resides.

Despite this often contrived collaborative presentation, the progressive pedagogy which is supported by many of the advocates of 'whole-language' approaches broadly advocates 'acquisition' of knowledge as opposed to the 'learning' of knowledge. Teachers seek to construct an environment where learning to read is acquired through more relaxed, meaningful and what is thought to be authentic contexts. Physical and intellectual space is provided within which children can exercise their right to choose the places, the people and the texts to utilize and enjoy. It can be argued that this form of pedagogy attempts to reconstruct an informal learning environment, similar to other informal environments outside school.

Visible and invisible pedagogy

Bernstein (2003) proposed that the 'the essential logic of any pedagogical relation consists of the relationship essentially between three rules' (p. 64) – *hierarchical, sequencing* and *criterial*. The hierarchical rule refers to the relationship between the transmitter and the acquirer (for example, teacher and student), a relationship governed by rules of social order, character and manner which condition the conduct of the pedagogic relation.

The sequential rules are the ordering and the pace by which the transmission is expected to be made. The criterial rules enable the acquirer to understand 'what counts as legitimate or illegitimate communications, social relations or position' (Bernstein 2003: 65) in the pedagogic relation. Bernstein classifies the hierarchical rules as *regulative* and the sequential and criterial *instructional* or *discursive*. These rules present the logic of relationships within any pedagogical situation and provide the means for the analysis of traditionalist and progressive methods of teaching.

Bernstein contended that there were two generic types of pedagogic practice. If the regulative and discursive rules are strong or explicit, he calls this type of pedagogy *visible* (VP). When the rules are implicit he calls this type of pedagogy *invisible* (IP). In Figure 7.1 Bernstein (2003) shows a typology of pedagogic styles. The vertical axis refers to the object of change of the pedagogic practice. The primary object will be to change the individual or to produce changes between social groups. The horizontal dimension refers to the focus of the pedagogic practice that may be upon the acquirer or the transmitter. The progressive and conservative (or traditional) pedagogies are situated above the horizontal. Both, according to Bernstein, are concerned with changing individuals but each demands a different role for the transmitter and the acquirer. Progressive models emphasize the 'acquisition' of knowledge; there is less of a direct instructional role for the teacher. The conservative, visible pedagogy provides a greater role on instruction or 'learning'.

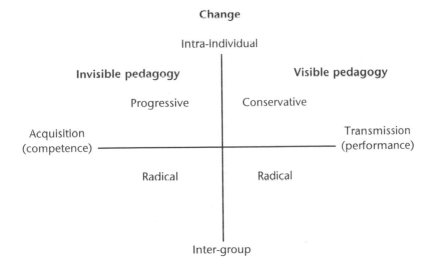

Figure 7.1: Typology of pedagogic styles
Source: Bernstein 2003

The top left-hand model fits well with the more 'progressive' whole-language approach to teaching reading. Bernstein describes this form of pedagogy as manifested in open spaces for the children with greater freedom of movement and where actions are largely unrestricted. The top right-hand 'conservative' or 'traditional' model fits well into contemporary skills-based instructional models for the teaching of reading. In this quadrant achievement is individualized and judged by the child's performance in the form of some mode of text. Classroom spaces are restricted and children's movement is often confined to the space around the table by which the child is sitting. There will be no expectation that children have choices about the learning, nor do the children have opportunities to lead the learning process. Lessons are tightly planned and executed by the teacher and success or failure is measured by strong criterial rules. Using this conceptual framework it is useful and insightful to examine practice in reading pedagogy. Macnair's teaching uses a visible pedagogy to teach reading, using synthetic phonics. It might be classed as broadly a visible pedagogy and Evans's classroom presents a more invisible pedagogy, with weaker hierarchical, criterial and sequential rules. These forms of reading pedagogy will be discussed later in this chapter.

Social class consciousness and reading

Bernstein spent most of his academic life attempting to understand the imbalance of achievement between social classes in schools. In doing so, he explored the social class assumptions that permeate the pedagogies employed in classrooms. Here I wish to discuss the nature of social class and social reproduction.

Bourdieu and Passeron (1977), Apple (2004) and Bernstein (1990) all have demonstrated that schools are organized and run by the middle class, or, as Marxists would observe, by the more wealthy and powerful class (Rikowski 2001). Class is generally seen as the way different sections of society and cultures are organized within the social and economic order. In the present circumstances this order is run as a system of capitalism. Members of this society are 'socialized into accepting the norms, values and customs of the social systems in which we grow up and schools have traditionally played a major part in this process' (Cole 2006: 4). Vygotsky's theory of semiotic mediation, as discussed earlier, is a powerful way of helping to understand these processes at a micro, individual, psychological level – how ways of being are constructed and sustained and the differences between different sections of society. Indeed, Vygotsky was a revolutionary Marxist himself. From a Marxist perspective:

In every society production is organized according to some division of labour, usually implying the division of society into classes having unequal responsibilities and rights ... All societies known to us in history have consisted of classes having different functions in the processes of production, distribution and consumption. Furthermore these have always involved imbalances of power: hence the description of history as the history of class struggle.

(Small 2005: 56-7)

Ball's (2003) conception of class is linked to subjective identity based on modes of being and becoming that are realized and reproduced in specific places. In other words we 'do' (Connell 1983) class – a dynamic process that is realized and struggled over in everyone's daily life. Class exists in our work, our pastimes and the texts we choose to read and immerse ourselves in. This more postmodernist subjective conception of class has been questioned by some (McLaren *et al.* 2002). McLaren *et al.* write that class 'has an objective existence as an empirical category and a subjective existence in terms of the ways in which it is lived' (2004: 46). However, for Ball, like McLaren, class is manifested starkly within educational settings, and the choices and actions that are made by parents and children within these environments have defining social consequences for the children concerned. Marxists would argue that it is in the interests of the ruling class that these divisions in society are maintained. This division of society contributes to clear distinctions in the way people develop and function and how cultures are developed and reproduced. Of course, schools do not have to be places where social reproduction is played out (Cole 2006) to maintain the social and economic order of society. Yet given the wealth of scholarship (Rikowski 2001; Ball 2003; Ball and Vincent 2005; Hatcher 2006) that suggests it can serve this purpose, as educationalists, an awareness of its contribution towards underachievement for large groups of children in all areas of schooling can be nothing other than crucial.

As Apple explains, Bourdieu argues

that the cultural capital stored in schools acts as an effective filtering device in the reproduction of the hierarchical society ... They take the cultural capital, the habitus, of the middle class, as natural and employ it as if all children have had equal access to it.

(Apple 2004: 31)

By 'cultural capital' Bourdieu means certain kinds of prior knowledge, abilities and language forms that are 'acquired' in particular cultures within society. It is the middle-class consciousness and capital that is favoured in schools and therefore, arguably, restricts those from other cultures who do not possess it from achieving the 'success' that school can offer. Following this argument, social reproduction processes occur as schools consecrate privilege and turn it into what is deemed to be merit. With this view one is forced to ask: 'What are advocates of specific forms of pedagogy actually trying to do?' To try and answer this question, Bernstein describes the social class assumptions of pedagogies which can be applied to what scholars and teachers are advocating for reading.

Social class assumptions of the pedagogies of reading

Bernstein (1990, 2003) was not a Marxist. However, he saw pedagogic practice as a form of cultural relay:

> A uniquely human device for both the reproduction and production of culture ... The relationship basic to cultural reproduction or transformation is essentially the pedagogic relation, and the pedagogic relation consists of transmitters and acquirers.
>
> (2003: 63–4)

Yet, in terms of the teaching of reading, which pedagogy – progressive and 'invisible' pedagogy (whole-language approaches), or traditional and 'visible' pedagogy (traditional instruction) – will benefit all, or, perhaps more importantly, those sections of society who regularly underachieve in school and in learning to read whom Gee (2001) highlights at the beginning of this chapter? As I will show, Bernstein reveals that despite each side's passionate belief in the efficacy of their pedagogy, its attachment to the middle-class culture from which it has derived cannot be shaken off and each pedagogy, whether progressive or traditional, has its home and consequently its success mainly within middle-class culture.

Bernstein disturbingly points out that, within the middle-class institutions of schools, principles and values are not always agreed upon. He brilliantly describes (2003) how factions of the middle class have been at loggerheads with each other over principles of social control that are a consequence of the pedagogies found in school. This assists in understanding the bitter debates over reading that continue to rage within education circles. Bernstein shows that the progressive *and* traditional pedagogues are mostly drawn from certain sections of the middle class. He differentiates between these sections and the pedagogy that they advocate, from one (the traditional) that is dependent on the economic market and emphasizes vocational education to the other that is opposed to market forces and advocates an education free from concerns about vocation and the economy (Sadovnik 2001). It is worth quoting Bernstein at length here:

> On the whole the middle-class sponsors of invisible pedagogy support state intervention and the expansion of agents and agencies of symbolic control, and thus the growth in public expenditure. For this is the ground and opportunity of their own reproduction and advancement, whereas the middle-class sponsors of visible pedagogy drawn from the economic sector and the entrepreneurial professions are opposed to growth in public expenditure. Thus there are opposing material and symbolic (discursive) interests.
>
> (Bernstein 2003: 212)

Within the middle class there are conflicting ideas on the basic principles of education and its ultimate aims and objectives. The debates about how to teach reading, therefore, lie within these conflicts of interest. But despite these differences, the logic of their principles rests within the middle class and its culture. According to Bernstein, each faction of this class maintains its persistent drive for social reproduction. In doing so, their pedagogies undermine the advancement of other cultures, namely those of the more oppressed classes. Educational debates and practices continue, mediated by middle class consciousness and culture. Recent history shows the rise and fall of both progressive and traditional pedagogies, as the factions of the middle class who have power within education policy wax and wane. This phenomenon is often described metaphorically as a pendulum that swings to and fro from progressive back to conservative pedagogies. An example of this is the focus and encouragement of creativity in schools (DfES 1999, 2003) which has been seen by many 'progressive' educationalists as a welcome respite from more prescriptive and 'visible' pedagogies demonstrated, for example, by the National Literacy Strategy (DfEE 1998). All the time the divisions and imbalance of power in society remain constant.

As someone who considers himself to be a 'progressive' educationalist, I found myself personally surprised after reading this conceptualization of the power relations and struggles in educational debates. Yet, at the same time I am intrigued by Bernstein's thesis and the way, one could argue, it shows the importance of political action to remove the roots of inequality permanently. Bernstein goes on to explain how these pedagogies produce these undermining effects on the oppressed classes.

Visible disadvantage: time and space

Bernstein's analysis of the social class assumptions of teaching practice links the micro-educational processes to the macro-sociological aspects of the social structure of society (Sadovnik 2001): 'Bernstein contributed to a greater understanding of how schools reproduce what they are ideologically committed to eradicating – social-class advantages in schooling and society' (Sadovnik 2001: 17).

According to Bernstein, the disadvantages of more dominated groups within society derive from issues of time and physical and cultural space. Using visible pedagogy, sequencing rules are explicit and clearly mark the future of the child's development in demarcated steps. The pace of this sequence is often consistently brisk. Here, oppressed groups are disadvantaged on two crucial fronts – lack of orientation to linguistic styles in the pedagogic community and the means to continue this form of literacy at home. As seen earlier in Macnair's (Macnair *et al.* 2006) description of her fast-paced phonics teaching, traditional forms of the teaching of reading require that the children quickly adjust to the new linguistic demands of learning to read. Children from homes where literacy events are more consistent with schooled literacies will have been introduced to this form of language use. 'The pacing rule of transmission acts selectively on those who acquire the school's pedagogic code, and this is a social class principle of selection' (Bernstein 2003: 73). This disadvantage, in terms of what Gee (2004) calls the primary discourses means that the children from homes where the discourse does not match those of school will require more time and greater determination to 'tune in' to the powerful discourses associated with academic success. The pace of the pedagogy is so great that there is a tendency for these children to lag behind others. There are real dangers that differences begin to emerge very quickly between groups of children who already understand these linguistic demands and those who do not. Skills-based teaching, as we have seen, is fast-paced with frequent tests and with homework demands.

Bernstein contended that for the academic curriculum to be acquired there need to be two sites of acquisition – school and home. This supplementation to the school day in the form of homework requires an appropriate space and a commitment and understanding of the pedagogy applied. Some homes, often from poorer families, do not have the economic capital to provide these resources and therefore 'failure becomes an expectation and the reality' (Bernstein 2003: 72). The 'learning' of knowledge associated with more traditional methods of the teaching of reading appears to fail to take these significant factors into account. Consequently, the same patterns of underachievement continue to be recorded.

Invisible disadvantage: space and lack of instruction

With the use of invisible pedagogic relations, inequalities also persist. For invisible pedagogy, cultural spaces and the freedom of movement and greater choice can also disadvantage some social groups. Bernstein argued that, despite its disadvantages described above, the surface features of visible pedagogy can be understood by many. It is a standard pedagogic form, often replicated in many family homes. Bernstein has always been clear that pedagogy occurs in many sites and is not unique to school and other official educational institutions. The home is also a key site of pedagogical relations. Bernstein describes pedagogy thus:

> Pedagogy is a sustained process whereby somebody(s) acquires new forms or develops existing forms of conduct, knowledge, practice and criteria, from somebody(s) or something deemed to be an appropriate provider or evaluator.
>
> (Bernstein 1999: 259)

For example, where space in the family house is restricted, each room tends to have a specific function and within these rooms, objects may have fixed positions and spaces may be reserved for people or things. Bernstein compares this special formation as linked to a visible pedagogic style. In more traditional teaching, as has been shown, children have many more restrictions on their movement. The children's day is planned rigorously with a regularity of procedures, as was demonstrated by Macnair's (Macnair *et al.* 2006) 'blueprint' for her reading lessons.

In homes with a more invisible pedagogy operating, space is more weakly demarcated. The rules that regulate the movement of things are less constraining. Living may be more open plan. Like the home operating a visible pedagogy, Bernstein argues, cognitive and social messages are carried by the spaces that are created or restricted. Invisible pedagogies both in school and in home require more space and they presuppose more movement by those concerned.

> When the spatial requirement is translated into family space it is
> clear that the family cannot employ an invisible pedagogy
> where there are members confined to a small space, as is the case
> with many working class and lower-working class families.
>
> (Bernstein 2003: 75)

Furthermore, families that need to operate visible pedagogies at home
punctuate time by a series of dislocations and expected behaviours.
Invisible pedagogies offer a very different temporal grid which may
appear alien to children from homes where time is treated very
differently and is more explicitly controlled (Lambirth 2006). Evans's
class, described earlier, has on the surface weaker hierarchical, sequential
and criterial rules which may be culturally more familiar to children
from more wealthy homes. In their efforts to make an environment
where knowledge can be 'acquired' rather than 'learned', the environment constructed is one that relays messages more associated with
teachers' own family homes and therefore the *acquisition* of knowledge is
less likely to occur for a large group of children.

Lack of instruction

Invisible pedagogy that is competence-orientated and intra-individual
(top left-hand quadrant in Figure 7.1) is described by Bernstein as being a
'masked pedagogy'. Although these pedagogic formulations appear to
provide weak selection, pacing and sequencing rules, and whilst children
are given more choice and autonomy, developmental learning theories
also require teachers to covertly evaluate children's productions against
selected fixed norms of attainment. The responsibility for success or
failure is given to the child. The child provides evidence of this by his or
her independent behaviour. This is taken as evidence of the child's
natural capacities (Bourne 2004). In this environment, in effect,
evaluation replaces instruction and deprives children of key aspects of
cultural capital, which children from dominated classes are unlikely to
find at home. Here again, following the argument, the middle class are
given an advantage. Important forms of cultural capital have been
provided by cultures whose literacy practices are more similar to those of
the school. This is not necessarily provided through instruction (or
indeed synthetic phonics) but, instead, acquired through regular
interaction with texts that match those found and valued in schools.
Reading is a cultural act that, Gee (2004) maintains, is developed more
effectively through acquisition than through instruction. Yet, in order to
acquire these forms of cultural capital a setting similar to the home

environments of the learners is of particular importance. However, the alternative model of explicit instruction, as advocated by the tradition-alists, creates other problems and disadvantages that have been discussed earlier on. Both learning through *acquisition* and learning through *instruction,* according to Bernstein's position, seem to provide challenges for children from working-class cultures. Education and the teaching of reading is a cultural act and therefore will privilege some and deny others.

Postmodern dilemmas – radical answers

The main thrust of this argument can be judged as deriving its conceptual framework from postmodern theory. Its emphasis upon the oppression of a culture through language may be perceived as being influenced and supported by postmodernist thinkers and educational-ists. Yet, my intention is to use these theoretical positions to argue for political change. As McLaren and Farahmandpur write:

> ... post-modern dissent is symptomatic of the structural contra-dictions and problematic assumptions within post-modern theory itself. By too often displacing critique to a field of serial negation without fully grasping its prefigurative or emancipatory potential, post-modern criticism frequently traps intelligibility and meaning internally, that is, inside the texts of culture.
>
> (McLaren and Farahmandpur 2002: 45–6)

The suggestion that working-class culture is repeatedly and system-atically undermined by the pedagogies of school culture demands attention by those concerned with education. But what also needs to be understood is that this has its roots in the social and economic system that, Marxists would argue, demands the subordination of one class by another. The pedagogies of reading reflect this political and economic state of affairs. Pedagogy must favour the cultures and semiotic backgrounds of the middle class in order to reproduce the class nature of society. Of course, some families from dominated classes can become aware of the need to acquire the cultural capital valued by society; but what is more important, from a Marxist position, is that the working class recognize their own power and organize to transform society into a truly democratic and equal one free from capitalism and the exploitation which is endemic in its function.

The pedagogies of reading and the debates that surround them need to be understood from micro and macro perspectives. Underachievement and the slower development in learning to read, on the whole, is found mainly in children from oppressed and subordinated groups, as Gee (2004) contends. The struggle to learn to read can be conceptualized as a symptom of the wider inequalities of society. As the pedagogic pendulum continues to swing from progressive to conservative and back again, arguably the class nature of society remains constant and, until this is rectified, underachievement for the working class will continue. This is not a negative message; on the contrary, this should provide progressive educationalists with a revolutionary optimism for the future emancipation of society. Those who campaign and struggle to improve the education of subordinated groups play a crucial role. As Rosa Luxemburg wrote at the end of the nineteenth century, 'Between social reforms and revolution there exists for the social democracy an indissoluble tie. The struggle for reforms is its means; the social revolution, its aim' (1970: 8). However, well-meaning pedagogies and reforms within traditional educational domains from the middle class who do not have these ultimate aims can, arguably, only continue to reproduce these inequalities, with the token exceptions of a relatively few children. In effect, they contribute to the maintenance of the existing order. Learning to read occurs in a cultural and political context. Bernstein's conceptualization of the class assumptions of pedagogy should lead to a tightening of the resolve of reading teachers to use their methods as a means to political change and a fairer society.

References

Apple, M. (2004) *Ideology and Curriculum,* 3rd edition. New York: RoutledgeFalmer.

Ball, S. J. (2003) *Class Strategies and the Education Market: The Middle Classes and Social Advantage.* London: RoutledgeFalmer.

Ball, S. J. and Vincent, C. (2005) 'Making up' the middle-class child: families, activities and class dispositions'. Paper prepared for BERA Conference, September, University of Glamorgan.

Barton, D. (1994) *Literacy: An Introduction to the Ecology of Written Language.* Oxford: Blackwell.

Beckett, F. (2000) 'Couldn't do better', *Guardian Education,* 19 September.

Bernstein, B. (1990) *The Structuring of Pedagogic Discourse, Volume IV: Class, Codes and Control.* London: Routledge.

Bernstein, B. (1996) *Pedagogy, Symbolic Control and Identity: Theory, Research, Critique.* London: Taylor and Francis.

Bernstein, B. (1990) *The Structuring of Pedagogic Discourse, Volume IV: Class, Codes and Control.* London: Routledge.

Bernstein, B. (1996) *Pedagogy, Symbolic Control and Identity*. London: Taylor and Francis.

Bernstein, B. (1999) Vertical and horizontal discourse: an essay, *British Journal of the Sociology of Education*, 20 (2): 157–73.

Bernstein, B. (2000) *Pedagogy, Symbolic Control and Identity: Theory, Research, Critique* (revised edition). Oxford: Rowman and Littlefield.

Bernstein, B. (2003) 'Social class and pedagogic practice', in *The Structuring of Pedagogic Discourse, Volume IV: Class, Codes and Control*. London: Routledge.

Bourdieu, P. and Passeron, J. C. (1977) *Reproduction in Education, Society and Culture*. London: Sage Publications.

Bourne, J. (2004) Framing talk: towards a 'radical visible pedagogy', in J. Muller, B. Davies and A. Morais (eds) *Reading Bernstein, Researching Bernstein*. London: RoutledgeFalmer.

Brice Heath, S. (1983) *Ways With Words: Language, Life, and Work in Communities and Classrooms*. New York: Cambridge University Press.

Cole, M. (2006) Introduction: human rights, equality and education, in M. Cole (ed.) *Education, Equality and Human Rights: Issues of Gender, 'Race', Sexuality, Disability and Social Class*, 2nd edition. Abingdon: Routledge.

Coles, G. (2000) *Misreading Reading: The Bad Science that Hurts Children*. Portsmouth, NH: Heinemann.

Connell, R. W. (1983) *Which Way is Up? Essays on Class, Sex, and Culture*. Sydney: Allen and Unwin.

Denny, C. and Elliott, L. (2004) The uphill struggle against poverty, *Guardian*, 31 March.

DfEE (1998) *The National Literacy Strategy*. London: DfEE.

DfEE (1999) *All Our Futures: Creativity, Culture and Education*. London: DfEE.

DfEE (2000) 'Inner-city schools improve faster to narrow the literacy and numeracy gap as test results confirm government target, DfEE press release, 20 September.

DfES (2003) *Excellence and Enjoyment: A Strategy for Primary Schools*. Nottingham: DfES.

DfES (Department for Education and Skills) (2004) *Five Year Strategy for Children and Learners*. London: HMSO.

DfES (2006) *Primary National Strategy*. Nottingham: DfES.

Foot, P. (2003) Adding up to much less, *Guardian*, 26 November.

Gee, J. P. (2001) What is literacy, in P. Shannon (ed.) *Becoming Political Too: New Readings and Writings on the Politics of Literacy Education*. Portsmouth NH: Heinemann.

Gee, J. P. (2004) *Situated Language and Learning: A Critique of Traditional Schooling*. Oxfordshire: Routledge.

Giroux, H. (1997) *Pedagogy and the Politics of Hope: Theory, Culture, and Schooling.* Oxford: Westview.

Giroux, H. (2005) *Schooling and the Struggle for Public Life: Democracy's Promise and Education's Challenge.* Boulder, CO: Paradigm Publishers.

Gramsci, A. (1971) *Selections from Prison Notebooks,* edited and translated by Q. Hoare and G. Smith. New York: International Publishers.

Hall, N. (1987) *The Emergence of Literacy.* London: Hodder and Stoughton.

Hasan, R. (2004) The concept of semiotic mediation: perspectives from Bernstein's sociology in J. Muller, B. Davies and A. Morais (eds) *Reading Bernstein, Researching Bernstein.* London: RoutledgeFalmer.

Hatcher, R. (2006) Social class and schooling: differentiation or democracy, in M. Cole (ed.) *Education, Equality and Human Rights: Issues of Gender, 'Race', Sexuality, Disability and Social Class,* 2nd edition. Abingdon: Routledge.

Hill, D. and Cole, M. (eds) (2001) *Schooling and Equality: Fact, Concept and Policy.* London: Kogan Page.

Jenkins, R. (1992) *Pierre Bourdieu.* London: Routledge.

Krashen, S. and Terrell, T. (1983) *The Natural Approach: Language Acquisition in the Classroom.* Hayward, CA: Alemany Press.

Lambirth, A. (2006) *Basil Bernstein (1924–2000) Thinking the Unthinkable for Ourselves: Lessons for Student Teachers and Student Educators,* TTRB Educational Thinkers Series, http://www.ttrb.ac.uk, May.

Lankshear, C. (1987) *Literacy, Schooling and Revolution.* Lewes: Falmer.

Luxemburg, R. (1970) *Reform or Revolution.* New York: Pathfinder Press.

McCallum, I. and Redhead, G. (2000) Poverty and educational performance, *Poverty,* 106: 14–17.

McLaren, P. and Farahmandpur, R. (2002) Breaking signifying chains: a Marxist position on postmodernism, in D. Hill, P. McLaren, M. Cole and G. Rikowski (eds) *Marxism against Postmodernism in Educational Theory,* Lanham, MD: Lexington Books.

Macnair, L. Evans, S., Perkins, M. and Goodwin, P. (2006) Inside the classroom: three approaches to phonics teaching, in M. Lewis and S. Ellis (eds) *Phonics: Practice, Research and Policy.* London: Sage Publications.

Marsh, J. (2006) Involving parents and carers, in M. Lewis and S. Ellis (eds) *Phonics: Practice, Research and Policy.* London: Sage Publications.

RRF (Reading Reform Foundation) (2006) www.rrf.org.uk/ Accessed September 2006.

Rikowski, G. (2001) The importance of being a radical educator in capitalism today, Guest Lecture presented to Sociology of Education Conference, Gillian Rose Room, University of Warwick, Coventry, 31 May, available from Institute for Education Policy Studies.

Rose, J. (2006) *An Independent Review of the Teaching of Early Reading.* Nottingham: DfES.

Routman, R. (1996) *Literacy at the Crossroads: Critical Talk about Reading and Writing, and Other Teaching Dilemmas.* Portsmouth, NH: Heinemann.

Sadovnik, A. R. (1995) Bernstein's theory of pedagogic practice, in A.R. Sadovnik (ed.) *Knowledge and Pedagogy: The Sociology of Basil Bernstein.* New Jersey, NJ: Ablex Publishing.

Sadovnik, A.R. (2001) Basil Bernstein (1924–2000): sociologist, mentor and friend, in S. Power, P. Aggleton, J. Brannen, A. Brown, L. Chisholm and J. Mace (eds) *A Tribute to Basil Bernstein 1924–2000.* London: Institute of Education.

Small, R. (2005) *Marx and Education.* Hampshire: Ashgate.

Smith, G., Smith, T. and Wright, G. (1997) (eds) *Britain Divided: The Growth of Social Exclusion in the 1980s and 1990s.* London: Child Poverty Action Group.

Stanovitch, K.E. (1993) Romance and reality, *Reading Teacher,* 47 (December/January): 280–91.

Street, B. (1984) *Literacy in Theory and Practice.* Cambridge: Cambridge University Press.

Sylva, K., Melhuish, E., Sammons, P., Siraj-Blatchford, I., Taggert, B. and Elliot, K. (2003) *The Effective Provision of Pre-School Education (EPPE).* London: Institute of Education/DfEE.

Taylor, D. (1997) Preamble in D. Taylor (ed.) *Many Families, Many Literacies: An International Declaration of Principles.* Portsmouth, NH: Heinemann.

Thomas, S. (2000) Overall patterns of achievement. Unpublished working paper on school effectiveness.

Vygotsky, L.S. (1978a) *Thought and Language.* Cambridge, MA: MIT Press.

Vygotsky, L.S. (1978b) *Mind in Society: The Development of Higher Psychological Processes.* Cambridge, MA: Harvard University Press.

Vygotsky, L.S. (1981) The genesis of higher mental functioning, in J.V. Wetsch (ed.) *The Concept of Activity in Soviet Psychology.* Armonk: Sharp.

8 Learning to read across languages: the role of phonics and synthetic phonics

Usha Goswami

When spoken language is represented by visual symbols, and we access meaning from decoding these symbols, we call it reading. Meaning is communicated by print instead of by speech. Different languages have invented different symbol systems (orthographies) for representing the spoken form. Most Western European languages use an alphabetic orthography. Languages like Korean, Hindi, Chinese and Japanese do not. For example, Chinese and Japanese use character-based scripts. All these types of visual symbol share one core feature. They can be recoded into sound. Teaching children 'phonics' provides direct instruction in how to achieve this recoding to sound. Phonics instruction teaches children how the visual symbol system of their language represents the sounds of the words in their language.

Phonics methods are not universal across languages, because the differences between orthographies are not merely visual. Orthographies also differ in the units of sound that they represent. This can be termed a difference in psycholinguistic 'grain size' (Ziegler and Goswami 2005, 2006). Chinese characters (called *Kanji*) represent the grain size of whole words. Japanese characters (called *Kana*) represent the grain size of individual syllables. The alphabet used in European languages usually represents the grain size of the phoneme. Phonemes are the smallest units of sound (phonology) that change the meaning of spoken words. For example, **cat** and **cap** differ in terms of the final phoneme. **Cat** and **cut** differ in terms of the medial phoneme.

Clearly, in order to teach a child to read a particular language, we need to teach them the correspondences between the orthographic symbols and the phonological grain size that those symbols represent. For many alphabetic languages, this can be achieved by a method called 'synthetic phonics'. In some European languages, the mapping from letter to phoneme is 1:1. Examples are Italian, Greek and Spanish. These languages are especially amenable to instruction based on synthetic phonics alone. This is not merely because of the 1:1 relation between letters and sounds, but also because the sound patterns of the words in these languages are easy to segment. Words in Italian and Spanish typically follow a CVCV (consonant–vowel–consonant–vowel) pattern. In other European languages, one letter can make more than one sound. Examples are English, Danish and French. For example, the letter A in English makes different sounds in the highly familiar words **cat**, **make**, **car**, and **talk**. The sound patterns of words in these languages are also more complex. For example, English has many CVC, CCVC and CVCC words. Such languages may require phonics to be taught at more than one psycholinguistic grain size.

In this chapter, I will argue that education must pay attention both to cross-language similarities and to cross-language differences in the psycholinguistic demands made by literacy. These similarities and differences are important for making decisions about how to teach phonics to beginning readers. The essential claim will be that whereas teaching 'synthetic phonics' may be very effective for languages like Italian, it may be only one phonics teaching method among many that are useful for a language like English.

Phonological awareness and learning to read

One cross-language similarity in the demands made by acquiring literacy is the central importance of 'phonological awareness'. Phonological awareness refers to a child's ability to detect and manipulate the component sounds that comprise words, at the different psycholinguistic grain sizes of syllable, onset-rime and phoneme. An important level of phonological awareness for literacy acquisition in languages like English is awareness of 'onset-rime' units. *Onsets* and *rimes* represent a phonological grain size intermediate between syllables and phonemes. The primary phonological processing unit across the world's languages is the syllable. Each syllable comprising a word can then be decomposed into onsets, rimes and phonemes in a hierarchical fashion. This is shown in Figure 8.1. The onset-rime division of the syllable depends on dividing at the vowel. For English, words like **sing**, **sting** and **spring** all share the same rime, the sound made by the letter string 'ing'. The onset of **sing** is /s/, the onset of **sting** is /st/, and the onset of **spring** is /spr/. These onsets comprise one, two and three phonemes respectively.

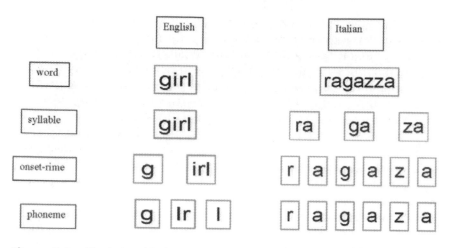

Figure 8.1: The heirarchical structure of the syllable, illustrated schematically via the word 'girl' in English and Italian

However, in many languages in the world, syllable structure is simple. Syllables are CV (consonant–vowel) units. Hence for many languages, onsets, rimes and phonemes are equivalent. Each onset and each rime in the syllable is also a single phoneme. This is illustrated for the Italian word 'ragazza'.

Research data collected across languages suggest that the development of phonological awareness follows a very similar developmental sequence. First, children gain awareness of syllables. Next, children gain awareness of onset-rime units. The relevant data have been reviewed in detail elsewhere (e.g. Ziegler and Goswami 2005). Eventually, and usually in response to direct teaching, children gain awareness of phonemes. A child's ability to reflect on the sound structure of the words used very efficiently in everyday communication thus develops quite gradually. Because of this, phonological awareness is also called *metalinguistic* awareness. Invoking 'meta' knowledge highlights the fact that the child needs to become consciously aware of information that is already present in the mental lexicon.

Becoming aware of phonemes

Cross-language differences in the psycholinguistic demands made by literacy appear to begin with the acquisition of phoneme awareness. Although some children in some studies in some languages (e.g. Turkish, Czech: see Ziegler and Goswami 2006) have been reported to develop some phoneme awareness prior to schooling, in general phoneme awareness develops as a result of direct teaching, usually the direct teaching of literacy. This is not particularly surprising, as the phoneme is not a natural speech unit, but an abstraction from the physical stimulus. For example, the 'a' phoneme in **bat** and **bag** is not exactly the same physical sound, and neither is the 'p' phoneme in **pit** and **spoon**. The mechanism for learning about these abstract units seems to be learning about letters. Letters are used to symbolize phonemes. Accordingly, the development of phonemic awareness depends in part on the consistency with which letters symbolize phonemes in different languages. This leads to cross-language divergence in the rate of development of phonemic awareness.

One task used across languages to measure the development of phoneme awareness is phoneme counting. When phoneme counting tasks are given to kindergarten children, there are notable cross-language differences in accuracy. German children perform at 51 per cent correct (Wimmer *et al.* 1991), French children at 2 per cent correct (Demont and Gombert 1996), Norwegian children at 56 per cent correct (Hoien *et al.* 1995) and Turkish children at 67 per cent correct (Durgunoglu and Oney 1999). One reason for this variability across languages is that not all of the studies of kindergartners checked that all of the participants were pre-readers. The words used in the different languages were not matched for difficulty either. However, perhaps a more important reason is that the written languages varied in orthographic consistency. English is a language with a particularly high degree of orthographic inconsistency. In English, counting tasks at the phoneme level are performed particularly poorly. For example, Liberman *et al.* (1974) reported 0 per cent phoneme awareness for English-speaking 4-year-olds, and 17 per cent phoneme awareness for English-speaking 5-year-olds.

By the end of first grade, children learning to read orthographically consistent languages typically score at high levels in phoneme awareness tasks. For example, Turkish children score 94 per cent correct, Greek children 100 per cent correct, and German children 92 per cent correct in the phoneme counting task (Durgunoglu and Oney 1999; Harris and Giannouli 1999; Wimmer *et al.* 1991). In contrast, studies of first grade (Year 2) English-speaking children by Tunmer and Nesdale (1985) and of second grade children by Perfetti *et al.* (1987) reported success levels of 71 per cent and 65 per cent respectively. Similarly, Demont and Gombert (1996) found that by the end of Grade 1, French children scored 61 per cent correct in phoneme counting tasks.

The relationship between phonological awareness and reading

Despite clear differences in the rate of acquisition of phoneme awareness, cross-language studies show that pre-school measures of phonological awareness predict reading and spelling development across languages. The measures of phonological awareness used in these longitudinal studies are usually syllable, onset and rime measures, because pre-schoolers are relatively young and usually cannot manage phoneme awareness tasks very well. Of course, there are lots of other cognitive variables that might cause a longitudinal relationship with reading. Examples are individual differences in intelligence, in memory, or in socio-economic status. Usually, these factors are also measured, and are then controlled in the longitudinal analyses. This enables the researchers to measure whether there is a *specific* connection between phonological awareness and progress in literacy.

Longitudinal connections between phonological awareness and literacy have been found in many languages. For example, Bradley and Bryant (1983) followed up 400 English pre-school children who had received an onset-rime measure of phonological awareness at ages 4 and 5 years. At follow-up, the children were aged on average 8 and 9 years. The children were given standardized tests of reading, spelling and reading comprehension, and their performance was adjusted for age and IQ. Bradley and Bryant found significant correlations between performance in the phonological task at ages 4 and 5 and reading and spelling performance three years later. Lundberg *et al.* (1980) gave 143 Swedish children a range of phonological awareness tests in kindergarten. The tests used included syllable blending, syllable segmentation, rhyme production, phoneme blending, phoneme segmentation and phoneme reversal. When the predictive relationships with reading attainment in second grade were measured, both the rhyme test and the phoneme tests were found to be significant predictors of reading.

In a German replication of the study by Lundberg *et al.* Wimmer *et al.* (1994) followed up 183 German kindergartners who had received an onset-rime measure at age 6 (in kindergarten) and tested their reading at 9 years 9 months. At this three-year follow-up, rime awareness was significantly related to both reading and spelling development. In a study with Norwegian pre-schoolers, Hoien *et al.* (1995) measured syllable, onset-rime and phoneme awareness in a sample of 128 6-year-olds. When reading was tested in first grade, individual differences in syllable, rhyme and phoneme awareness all made independent contributions to variance in reading. In a study with Chinese pre-schoolers reported by Ho and Bryant (1997), 100 Chinese children were given an onset-rime measure at age 3 years. When their progress in reading and spelling was measured two years later, phonological awareness was found to be a significant predictor of reading even after other factors such as age, IQ and mother's educational level had been controlled.

Individual differences in phonological sensitivity hence predict individual differences in reading attainment across languages, even for children who are learning to read non-alphabetic scripts. However, the existence of a robust longitudinal association between factor A (e.g. phonological awareness) and outcome B (e.g. literacy) does not in itself show a causal relationship. To explore causality, an intervention study is required. In the area of reading and spelling, there are now many such intervention studies, because improving children's literacy is an important goal for governments in many cultures. However, to be valid, an intervention study must employ a stringent research design (Goswami 2003). For example, it is important that the control group receives an intervention of equivalent intensity. When exploring causality, it is not sufficient to compare a group of children who receive a phonological intervention to a group of children who do not. Although the children in such 'unseen' control groups are receiving training from their classroom teachers, they are not receiving individualized attention from a motivated researcher who is piloting a special new training programme. Effects due simply to participating in an intervention are called 'Hawthorne' effects. They arise not from cognitive changes due to targeted training, but from the generalized motivational and self-esteem effects of participating in something extra and unusual.

Unfortunately, there are rather few training studies in the literature that have utilized a stringent research design. Nevertheless, when we restrict ourselves to considering only well-designed studies, we find another cross-language similarity in the factors determining reading acquisition. Providing training in phonological awareness, particularly when coupled with training in how different phonological grain sizes are linked to print, improves reading outcomes across languages. This has been shown for English by Bradley and Bryant (1983), for Danish by Lundberg et al. (1988), and for German by Schneider et al. (1997, 2000).

Learning to decode in different languages

So far, we have seen that there are cross-language similarities in the role of phonological awareness in literacy acquisition, and in the early development of phonological awareness. Across languages, children develop syllable and onset-rime awareness prior to schooling, but there is divergence in the ease and rate of attainment of phoneme awareness. Psycholinguistic grain size theory (Ziegler and Goswami 2005, 2006) captures these similarities and differences by highlighting two important factors for early literacy acquisition. The first is the phonological structure of the syllable. For many of the world's languages, the most frequent syllable type is CV. For these languages, onset-rime segmentation of the syllable is equivalent to phonemic segmentation. Hence phoneme awareness is attained rapidly by children. Only 5 per cent of English monosyllables follow the CV pattern (see De Cara and Goswami 2002; examples are **go** and **see**).[1] The second important factor is orthographic consistency. As noted earlier, some languages have a 1:1 mapping between letters and sounds, like Spanish and Italian. These languages have orthographic consistency for reading. Other languages have a 1: many mapping between letters and sounds. These languages do not have orthographic consistency for reading. In a language like English, letters or letter clusters can be pronounced in more than one way. For example, O makes a different sound in **go** and **to**, EA makes different sound in **speak** and **steak**, and G makes a different sound in **magic** and **bag** (see Berndt *et al.* 1987; Ziegler *et al.* 1997).

According to psycholinguistic grain size theory, beginning readers across languages are faced with three problems: availability, consistency and the granularity of symbol-to-sound mappings. The *availability* problem reflects the fact that not all phonological units are accessible prior to reading. In particular, phonemes may be inaccessible to pre-readers, particularly in languages with a complex syllable structure. For these languages, the grain sizes that are available prior to reading (syllables and onset-rimes) may not correspond to the visual symbols used to represent phonology. The *consistency* problem refers to the fact that the alphabet represents phonemes with more consistency in some languages than in others. Italian, German and Spanish are all highly consistent in their spelling-sound correspondences. English, Danish and French are much less consistent in their spelling-sound correspondences. Young readers of English have to decode words like **though**, **cough**, **through** and **bough**.

Finally, the *granularity* problem refers to the fact that there are many more orthographic units to learn when access to the phonological system is based on bigger grain sizes as opposed to smaller grain sizes. That is, there are more words than there are syllables, there are more syllables than there are rimes, there are more rimes than there are graphemes, and there are more graphemes than there are letters (graphemes are alphabetic units that make a single sound, for example the phoneme /f/ can be represented by the grapheme 'ph'). Ziegler and Goswami argued that reading proficiency in a particular language will depend on the resolution of all three of these problems (Ziegler and Goswami 2005, 2006, for detail). For example, children learning to read English must develop multiple decoding strategies in parallel in order to become successful readers. They need to develop whole-word recognition strategies in order to read words like **cough** and **yacht**. They need to develop rhyme analogy strategies in order to read irregular words like **light**, **night** and **fight**. Finally, they need to develop grapheme–phoneme recoding strategies in order to read regular words like **cat**, **pen** and **big**.

As consistent orthographies (almost) only have regular words, a child needs merely to develop grapheme–phoneme recoding strategies in order to become a highly skilled reader. Children who are learning to read languages like German, Italian, Spanish and Finnish learn to read very successfully in letter-by-letter fashion. Indeed, a grapheme–phoneme recoding strategy develops to an efficient level within the first months of learning to read such languages (e.g. Cossu *et al.* 1995; Wimmer 1996; Durgunoglu and Oney 1999). It is also easy to teach reading in these languages, because 'synthetic phonics' will work for almost any word in the language. There are various experimental 'hallmarks' that are suggestive of a reliance on grapheme–phoneme recoding in children's reading. One is a length effect. Children who are reading by applying grapheme–phoneme correspondences should take longer to read words with more letters/phonemes. Children learning to read consistent orthographies like Greek show reliable length effects compared to children learning to read English (e.g. Goswami *et al.* 1997).

Another hallmark of grapheme–phoneme recoding is skilled non-word reading. Children who are applying grapheme–phoneme correspondences should be as efficient at reading letter strings that do not correspond to real words (e.g. **tix**, **segwump**) as they are at reading letter strings that do correspond to real words (**ball**, **wigwam**). Numerous experiments show that young readers of consistent orthographies like German are much better at reading matched non-words than English children (e.g. Frith *et al.* 1998). However, there is more than one way of reading a non-word. A non-word like **tix** can either be read by applying grapheme–phoneme correspondences, or can be read by analogy to a familiar real word like **six**. German children show no difference in reading accuracy for non-words that can be read by analogy compared to non-words that cannot be read by analogy. English children do show a difference. For example, Goswami *et al.* (2003) contrasted non-words that could be read by analogy to real English words (e.g. **dake** [cake], **murn** [burn]) to phonologically-matched non-words that required grapheme–phoneme recoding (e.g. **daik**, **mirn**). The English children found the analogy non-words (48 per cent correct) easier than the grapheme–phoneme non-words (38 per cent correct) when presentation was blocked by grain size. The German children read the two types of non-words (large grain size, small grain size) very efficiently, even when the non-words were mixed together into one list. This was interpreted as evidence that the German children were applying grapheme–phoneme recoding strategies to both types of non-words. The English children showed a strategy switching cost with the mixed list, making almost 20 per cent more errors when the non-words representing different grain sizes were mixed together.

Cross-language comparisons of decoding efficiency

As might be expected given the foregoing analysis, the rate at which children acquire grapheme–phoneme recoding strategies varies markedly with orthographic consistency. One large cross-language study compared children who were learning to read some of the different European Union languages during their first year of reading instruction. Scientists in 14 European Union countries measured simple word and non-word reading in first grade. The word and non-word items used were matched for difficulty across the languages. First-grade performance was studied in order to match the length of reading tuition across languages. Further, all participating children were attending schools using 'phonics'-based (grapheme–phoneme-based) instructional programmes (see Seymour *et al.* 2003). The ages of the participating children differed, however, as (for example) children in England and Scotland begin school at age 5, whereas Scandanavian children begin school at age 7. The data are shown in Table 8.1.

As can be seen, the efficiency of grapheme–phoneme recoding was remarkable during the first year of teaching for most of the European languages. Children learning to read languages like Finnish, German, Spanish and Greek showed accuracy levels above 90 per cent correct, for both words and non-words. In contrast, children learning to read languages with less orthographic consistency were less accurate in word and non-word reading. Languages like French (79 per cent correct), Danish (71 per cent correct) and Portuguese (73 per cent correct) all showed lower levels of decoding efficiency. The children learning to read in English showed the slowest rates of acquisition. They read 34 per cent of the simple words correctly and 29 per cent of the simple non-words. When followed up a year later, these children were achieving levels of around 70 per cent correct. This was still short of the early efficiency shown by the Italians and Germans.

These cross-language differences in the rate of acquisition are

Table 8.1: Data (percentage correct) from the COST A8 study of grapheme–phoneme recoding skills for monosyllables in 14 European languages (adapted from Seymour *et al.* 2003)

Language	Familiar real words	Non-words
Greek	98	97
Finnish	98	98
German	98	98
Austrian German	97	97
Italian	95	92
Spanish	95	93
Swedish	95	91
Dutch	95	90
Icelandic	94	91
Norwegian	92	93
French	79	88
Portuguese	73	76
Danish	71	63
Scottish English	34	41

unsurprising if we consider that English is a highly inconsistent orthography, and that English has a complex phonological structure. The variable spelling patterns of English words require flexibility in decoding strategies. For example, words such as **choir** have to be recognized as whole patterns. Words such as **light** are also irregular at the grapheme–phoneme level, but they have complete orthographic consistency at the rime level (**fight, sight, tight**). Such words can be decoded by rhyme analogy. Given these facts about English orthography and phonology, it seems unlikely that relying on one teaching method could lead to rates of acquisition comparable to those shown by Finnish, Italian and German children. Yet recently, claims have been made that one teaching method, labelled 'synthetic phonics', can indeed lead to remarkable gains in reading for English-speaking children (Johnston and Watson 2004). This method was highlighted by the Rose Review of the Teaching of Early Reading (Rose 2006). The Rose Review claimed that teaching 'synthetic phonics' in English classrooms would offer 'the vast majority of beginners the best route to becoming skilled readers' (p. 19). How strong is the evidence for this claim? To answer this question, we need empirical data.

Studies exploring synthetic phonics methods

One of the first studies investigating the potential benefits of synthetic phonics was carried out by Landerl (2000). She compared English children taught via a synthetic phonics programme (now called Jolly Phonics; Lloyd 1994) to English children receiving mixed methods or standard reading tuition, and she also included a group of German children taught by synthetic phonics methods in Germany. Landerl described the 'standard' mixed method of reading tuition (pre-National Literacy Strategy) as 'a mixed approach providing a combination of whole word and phonics methods' (p. 241) ... 'children in this school received a phonics lesson once a week' (p. 247). The outcome measure was the accuracy of reading non-words such as **tix** at grades 1, 2, 3 and 4 in each school.

I will focus on Experiment 2, as this was the only study for which Landerl herself carried out the testing of all participating children (Experiment 1 was a pilot study, in which teachers who were enthusiastic about synthetic phonics methods tested the synthetic phonics children in their school). For Experiment 2, Landerl herself tested 111 children following the mixed method of reading tuition in the 'English standard' school, 87 children in the synthetic phonics school, and 102 children in a German school. Non-word reading accuracy at Grades 1 (age 6) and 2 (age 7) was found to be equivalent for the two sets of English children. Both groups were significantly poorer than the German children. By Grade 3, non-word reading accuracy for English was much better, with 28 per cent errors for the mixed methods group and 7 per cent for the synthetic phonics group. By Grade 4, the difference between the two English groups had disappeared. Landerl concluded 'the English standard [mixed methods] children performed almost as well as the English phonics children [in the early grades]' (p. 250). This does not support the claim by Rose that synthetic phonics offers 'the vast majority of beginners' the best route to becoming skilled readers. In this study, the method of reading tuition made no difference to the efficiency of grapheme–phoneme recoding for English beginning readers (Grades 1 and 2).

A training study of beginning readers comparing two kinds of phonics tuition was reported by Walton et al. (2001). One type of phonics training was based on phonemes (called letter recoding) and the second used a larger phonological grain size (called rime analogy). These two training methods are characteristic of the wider literature comparing 'synthetic' with 'analytic' methods. This literature usually regards 'analytic' phonics as going from 'whole to part', focusing initially at larger grain sizes (Moustafa and Maldonado-Colon 1998). 'Synthetic' phonics is regarded as going from 'part to whole', focusing initially on the smallest grain size of the phoneme. The children studied by Walton *et al.* were pre-readers, and this was their first direct tuition in reading. Both experimental groups were taught the same pre-reading skills (phonological awareness of initial, medial and final phonemes, rhyming and the letter–sound correspondences). Two phonics training sessions of 25 minutes were given twice a week for 11 weeks. An unseen control group received no extra tuition.

When reading outcomes were assessed, the groups were found to have made broadly equivalent progress. For non-word reading, the two groups performed at the same level, while for word reading a significant advantage was found for the rime analogy group. In each case, the trained children outperformed the unseen control group, who had received normal classroom teaching. When longitudinal post-tests were administered four months later, the two training groups were still equivalent. This study is important, as the two phonics training programmes were controlled so that the only differences concerned whether the first steps of reading were taught using a letter–sound recoding strategy or a rime analogy strategy. The overwhelming finding was that both types of phonics were equally effective.

Logically, it is possible that teaching reading via synthetic phonics might lead to rates of acquisition comparable to those of Finnish, Italian and German children if cultural and other socio-economic differences were equated across languages. This can only be investigated in bilingual cultures, where everyone lives together and children differ only in the language of reading instruction. In Wales, children living in the same towns and villages grow up with either Welsh or English as their native tongue, and their parents can choose whether to have them schooled in Welsh or English. Welsh is a very transparent orthography, with unambiguous mappings from graphemes to phonemes. Like English, syllable structure is complex. Welsh syllables can have multi-phoneme onsets, as in **streic** and **cnau**, or codas, as in **sinc** and **peint**. Welsh thus differs from English in terms of one important factor, orthographic consistency, but not in terms of the other, syllable complexity. Spencer and Hanley (2003) therefore studied children living in Wales who were being taught to read either English or Welsh using phonics programmes (such as Jolly Phonics, a synthetic phonics programme, for English). The children were in their second year of formal reading instruction and were on average 6 years old.

Spencer and Hanley found that the English-speaking children were significantly less accurate in both word and non-word reading compared to the Welsh-speaking children. For real words, the English-speaking children read on average 59 per cent of words correctly, compared to 81 per cent correct for the Welsh-speaking children. For non-words, the English-speaking children read on average 44 per cent of words correctly, compared to 78 per cent correct for the Welsh-speaking children. The Welsh-speaking children had also developed superior phonemic awareness (measured by a phoneme counting task). Spencer and Hanley concluded that their findings 'provided strong evidence that reading acquisition is heavily influenced by the transparency of the alphabetic writing system' (p. 14). The children were followed up a year later, and the Welsh-speaking children were still significantly better at word reading, non-word reading and phoneme counting than the English-speaking children. At a second follow-up three years later, the differences between the Welsh-speaking and English-speaking children had disappeared (Hanley *et al.* 2004). By this time the children had had six years of formal reading instruction, and were now 10 years old. Again, this study suggests that teaching method *per se* is not the explanation for the slower acquisition of reading skills that characterizes English-speaking children. We must seek the causal factors elsewhere, in orthographic consistency and syllable complexity.

The 'Clackmannanshire' studies exploring synthetic phonics cited in the Rose Review

Despite these findings, Rose (2006) was very certain that the method adopted to teach phonics to English-speaking children could make a critical difference to acquisition (recall his claim that 'synthetic phonics offers the vast majority of beginners the best route to becoming skilled readers', p. 19). What was the evidence base for this conclusion? One source of evidence cited by Rose (2006) was not empirical at all, but concerned a visit by his team of inspectors to a Scottish education authority (Clackmannanshire) that used synthetic phonics methods. Rose wrote: 'The visit provided the review with first-hand evidence of very effective teaching and learning of phonic knowledge ... focusing on the practice observed in the classroom and its supportive context, rather than debating the research, is therefore not without significance for this review' (p. 62). He cited anecdotal evidence, too, for example: 'One teacher said "I have never seen results like this in thirty years of teaching"' (p. 63). Regarding empirical evidence, Rose took a more pessimistic view: 'In recent years, there has been a convergence of opinion among psychologists investigating reading that little progress towards understanding how reading happens in the human mind is likely to be made' (p. 75). Nevertheless, Rose did cite some empirical evidence. For example, he highlighted a series of research studies carried out in the same local education authority of Clackmannanshire.

These studies were carried out by Johnston and Watson, who made a series of astonishing claims for the reading progress that children achieved when following their version of a 'synthetic phonics' programme (Watson and Johnston 1998; Johnston and Watson 2003, 2004, 2005). The Rose review summarized these claims as follows:

> At the end of Primary 7 [Year 6 in England, i.e. age 10 to 11], word reading was 3 years 6 months ahead of chronological age, spelling was 1 year 8 months ahead and reading comprehension was 3.5 months ahead. However, as mean receptive vocabulary knowledge ... was 93 at the start of this study ... this may be an underestimate of the gains with this method.
>
> (p. 61)

Nevertheless, only one of the publications referred to has been published in a peer-reviewed journal (Johnston and Watson 2004). I will therefore focus on this paper in order to assess the empirical quality of the research designs upon which these claims depend. How stringent were these research designs?

Two studies were reported in the 2004 paper (Johnston and Watson 2004). In study 1, three groups of 5-year-old children were given different phonics training programmes by their teachers for 16 weeks. The programmes began two weeks after school entry, and replaced all phonics teaching normally carried out in the participating classrooms. One group was given the 'synthetic phonics' training programme for 20 minutes daily. 'In a synthetic phonics programme, children are taught letter sounds very rapidly, and after the first few letters have been taught they are shown how to blend or synthesize the sounds together to pronounce unfamiliar printed words; spelling is taught by means of phonemic analysis' (p. 330). Two letter sounds were taught in one day, in the beginning, middle and end positions of CVC (consonant–vowel–consonant) words. The children were trained to sound the letters and blend the letter sounds and to write the letters. As more letters were trained, plastic letters were used to create words, and the children sounded, blended and read the words comprising the target list. They also learned to spell the words from pictures.

The two other groups of 5-year-olds followed an 'analytic phonics' training programme. One group followed this programme for 10 minutes a day, spending the other 10 minutes analysing and blending oral sounds in the absence of letters, and the other group followed the programme for 20 minutes a day. Essentially, the 'analytic phonics' children were taught letter sounds in the context of learning sight words. Letters were taught at the rate of one letter a week. The teachers showed the children different words containing the taught letters in initial position (onset), and then read the words to the children. The children learned to match the target letters to the initial sounds of pictured words, and to write these letters in isolation, but they were not taught to read the words themselves. Clearly, these children were being taught much less about reading than those in the 'synthetic phonics' group. By the end of the 16 weeks of training, the analytic groups had only been taught 16 letters instead of 26 letters. Unlike the synthetic group, they had not been taught to decode simple words via CVC blending and decoding, and they had not been taught to write all 26 letters. They had not got through as many words either, so to 'ensure the children in the three groups received the same exposure to new print words' (p. 335), Johnston and Watson asked the teachers to read the children in the 'analytic' groups the rest of the words. This is not the same kind of 'exposure to new print words' as that given to the synthetic phonics group, who had been taught to blend and decode the letter sounds comprising the words using plastic letters, who had been taught all of the relevant letter sounds that made up the words, and who had been taught to spell the words when given pictures.

When the literacy skills of the three groups were compared, the synthetic phonics group knew 90 per cent of their letters on average, while the analytic phonics group knew around 58 per cent. This is completely unsurprising, as the synthetic phonics group had been taught all the letters and the analytic phonics groups had only been taught 60 per cent of the letters. In terms of progress in reading, the two analytic phonics groups (mean age 5 years 4 months) were found to have reading ages of 5 years 4 months on average. The synthetic phonics group (mean age 5 years 5 months) had a reading age of 6 years 0 months (a significant difference). Again, this is completely unsurprising. The synthetic phonics group had been taught much more extensive reading skills (e.g. sounding out, blending, spelling). Yet Johnston and Watson concluded: 'In Experiment 1, it was shown ... that synthetic phonics was more effective in developing reading, spelling and phonemic awareness ability than both analytic phonics [programmes]' (p. 351). This conclusion is not permissible, as the contrast between the different experimental conditions was not a pure contrast between 'synthetic' and 'analytic' *teaching methods*. Rather, the contrast between instructional method was confounded with the absolute amount taught. Study 1 cannot tell us whether it makes a difference to learning if phonics skills are taught analytically, from word to sound, or synthetically, from sound to word.

The second study in the paper suffered from similar problems. In this second study, training was administered by the authors, and was extra to normal classroom tuition. The extra training was given twice weekly for

10 weeks. There were two critical training groups, both of whom learned two letters per week. One group ('accelerated letter learning group') learned the letters in the initial position in words only, learned to match pictures and words, but were not taught to decode. The second group ('synthetic phonics group') learned the letters in all positions of words, learned to sound and blend using plastic letters, and were taught to read the 114 words used in the study for themselves. Again, outcomes were superior in the synthetic phonics group. Again, this is unsurprising. This group were taught much more extensive reading skills. They were taught letter–sound correspondences in all positions within words, they were taught to sound out words, and they were taught to blend phonemes. Yet Johnston and Watson concluded: 'Experiment 2 ... [controlled] for speed of letter learning; [yet] the synthetic phonics group still read and spelt better than the analytic phonics group. It is concluded that synthetic phonics was a more effective approach to teaching reading, spelling and phonemic awareness than analytic phonics' (p. 351).

Again, this conclusion is not justified. The design of the study does not enable the authors to draw a conclusion about the superiority of one phonics *teaching method* against another (synthetic versus analytic). The absolute amount taught to the children in each group differed markedly. In order to compare the relative value of analytic versus synthetic methods of teaching phonics, each group should be taught the same skills of sounding out, blending and decoding the 114 target words. The only difference should be whether this teaching occurs analytically, from word to sound, or synthetically, from sound to word. It is currently unknown whether any differences would be found if such a stringent research design were to be used in the Clackmannanshire studies. However, given the empirical studies reviewed earlier, it seems unlikely. In fact, the largest meta-analysis of different phonics training studies conducted to date, the US National Reading Panel (NRP) study, has already asked: 'Are some types of phonics instruction more effective than others? Are some specific phonics programmes more effective than others?'. The NRP study concluded that 'specific systematic phonics programs are all significantly more effective than non-phonics programs; however, they do not appear to differ significantly from each other in their effectiveness ...' (National Institute of Child Health and Human Development 2000: 93).

Conclusion

To date, there is no empirical evidence that justifies the Rose Review's conclusion that teaching synthetic phonics in English classrooms offers 'the vast majority of beginners the best route to becoming skilled readers' (Rose 2006: 19). Rather, there is a lot of evidence that supports the Rose Review's emphasis on the benefits of teaching phonics *systematically*. Phonics can be taught systematically in a variety of ways. Meanwhile, cross-language data offer some insights into why English is a relatively difficult language to learn to read. These insights are very useful for the teacher of phonics. The first is that English syllables are phonologically complex, and this matters for children's ease of learning. English does not follow a simple CV syllable structure, and so learning to segment words into phonemes is difficult, and onset-rime skills are important. The second is that the English orthography is very inconsistent. This is why phonics tuition should not focus exclusively at the grain size of the phoneme. There are important spelling consistencies at the level of onsets and rimes (Treiman *et al.* 1995). Further, words like **yacht** need to be learned as holistic patterns. In order to optimize the teaching of early reading in English, we need to take all of these factors into account. The design of instructional programmes for recoding visual symbols into sounds needs to reflect the cross-language empirical evidence base.

Note

[1] The most frequent syllable type in English is CVC (43 per cent of monosyllables, e.g. **cat**, **dog**, **soap**), and there are also many CCVC syllables (15 per cent of monosyllables, e.g. **trip**, **spin**), CVCC syllables (21 per cent of monosyllables, e.g. **fast**, **jump**), and some CCVCC syllables (6 per cent, e.g. **crust**).

References

Berndt, R. S., Reggia, J. A. and Mitchum, C. C. (1987) Empirically derived probabilities for grapheme-to-phoneme correspondences, *English. Behavior Research Methods, Instruments, & Computers*, 19: 1–9.

Bradley, L. and Bryant, P.E. (1983) Categorising sounds and learning to read: a causal connection, *Nature*, 310: 419–21.

Cossu, G., Gugliotta, M. and Marshall, J.C. (1995) Acquisition of reading and written spelling in a transparent orthography: two non-parallel processes?, *Reading and Writing*, 7: 9–22.

De Cara, B. and Goswami, U. (2002) Statistical analysis of similarity relations among spoken words: evidence for the special status of rimes, *English. Behavioural Research Methods and Instrumentation*, 34 (3): 416–23.

Demont, E. and Gombert, J.E. (1996) Phonological awareness as a predictor of recoding skills and syntactic awareness as a predictor of comprehension skills, *British Journal of Educational Psychology*, 66: 315–32.

Durgunoglu, A.Y. and Oney, B. (1999) A cross-linguistic comparison of phonological awareness and word recognition, *Reading and Writing*, 11: 281–99.

Frith, U., Wimmer, H. and Landerl, K. (1998) Differences in phonological recoding in German- and English-speaking children, *Scientific Studies of Reading*, 2: 31–54.

Goswami, U. (2003) Why theories about developmental dyslexia require developmental designs, *Trends in Cognitive Sciences*, Vol 7: 534–40.

Goswami, U., Porpodas, C. and Weelwright, S. (1997) Children's orthographic representations in English and Greek, *European Journal of Psychology of Education*, 3: 273–92.

Goswami, U., Ziegler, J. C., Dalton, L. and Schneider, W. (2003) Non-word reading across orthographies: how flexible is the choice of reading units?, *Applied Psycholinguistics*, 24: 235–47.

Hanley, R., Masterson, J., Spencer, L. and Evans, D. (2004) How long do the effects of learning to read a transparent orthography last? An investigation of the reading skills and reading impairment of Welsh children at 10 years of age, *Quarterly Journal of Experimental Psychology*, 57: 1393–410.

Harris, M. and Giannouli, V. (1999) Learning to read and spell in Greek: the importance of letter knowledge and morphological awareness, in M. Harris and G. Hatano (eds), *Learning to Read and Write: A Cross-Linguistic Perspective*. Cambridge: Cambridge University Press.

Ho, C. S.-H. and Bryant, P. (1997) Phonological skills are important in learning to read Chinese, *Developmental Psychology*, 33: 946–51.

Hoien, T., Lundberg, L., Stanovich, K.E. and Bjaalid, I.K. (1995) Components of phonological awareness, *Reading and Writing*, 7: 171–88.

Johnston, R.S. and Watson, J. (2003) Accelerating reading and spelling with synthetic phonics: a five-year follow up, *Insight 4*. Edinburgh: Scottish Executive Education Department.

Johnston, R.S. and Watson, J. (2004) Accelerating the development of reading, spelling and phonemic awareness skills in initial readers, *Reading and Writing*, 17: 327–57.

Johnston, R. and Watson, J. (2005) *The Effects of Synthetic Phonics Teaching on Reading and Spelling Attainment: A Seven Year Longitudinal Study*. Edinburgh: The Scottish Executive Central Research Unit. www.scotland.gov.uk/Resource/DOC/36496/0023582.pdf.

Landerl, K. (2000) Influences of orthographic consistency and reading instruction on the development of non-word reading skills, *European Journal of Psychology of Education*, 15: 239–57.

Liberman, I.Y., Shankweiler, D., Fischer, F.W. and Carter, B. (1974) Explicit syllable and phoneme segmentation in the young child, *Journal of Experimental Child Psychology*, 18: 201–12.

Lloyd, S. (1994) *The Phonics Handbook.* Chigwell: Jolly Learning.

Lundberg, I., Frost, J. and Petersen, O. (1988) Effects of an extensive programme for stimulating phonological awareness in pre-school children, *Reading Research Quarterly*, 23: 163–284.

Lundberg, I., Olofsson, A. and Wall, S. (1980) Reading and spelling skills in the first school years predicted from phonemic awareness skills in kindergarten, *Scandinavian Journal of Psychology*, 21: 159–73.

Moustafa, M. and Maldonado-Colon, E. (1998) Whole-to-parts phonics instruction: building on what children know to help them know more, *The Reading Teacher*, 52: 448–58.

National Institute of Child Health and Human Development (2000) *Report of the National Reading Panel. Teaching Children to Read: An Evidence-based Assessment of the Scientific Research Literature on Reading and its Implications for Reading Instruction: Reports of the Subgroups* (NIH publication no. 00-4754). Washington, DC: US Government Printing Office.

Perfetti, C.A., Beck, I., Bell, L. and Hughes, C. (1987) Phonemic knowledge and learning to read are reciprocal: a longitudinal study of first grade children, *Merrill-Palmer Quarterly*, 33: 283–319.

Rose, J. (2006) *An Independent Review of the Teaching of Early Reading.* Nottingham: DfES.

Schneider, W., Kuespert, P., Roth, E., Vise, M. and Marx, H. (1997) Short- and long-term effects of training phonological awareness in kindergarten: evidence from two German studies, *Journal of Experimental Child Psychology*, 66: 311–40.

Schneider, W., Roth, E. and Ennemoser, M. (2000) Training phonological skills and letter knowledge in children at-risk for dyslexia: a comparison of three kindergarten intervention programs, *Journal of Educational Psychology*, 92: 284–95.

Seymour, P.H.K., Aro, M. and Erskine, J.M. (2003) Foundation literacy acquisition in European orthographies, *British Journal of Psychology*, 94: 143–74.

Spencer, L.H. and Healey, J.R. (2003) Effects of orthographic transparency on reading and phoneme awareness in children learning to read in Wales, *British Journal of Psychology*, 94 (1): 1–28.

Treiman, R., Mullennix, J., Bijeljac-Babic, R. and Richmond-Welty, E. D. (1995) The special role of rimes in the description, use, and acquisition of English orthography, *Journal of Experimental Psychology: General*, 124: 107–36.

Tunmer, W.E. and Nesdale, A.R. (1985) Phonemic segmentation skill and beginning reading, *Journal of Educational Psychology*, 77: 417–27.

Walton, P. D., Walton, L.M. and Felton, K. (2001) Teaching rime analogy or letter recoding reading strategies to pre-readers: effects on pre-reading skill and word reading, *Journal of Educational Psychology*, 93(1): 160–80.

Watson, J.E. and Johnston, R.S. (1998) *Accelerating Reading Attainment: The Effectiveness of Synthetic Phonics*, Interchange 57. Edinburgh: SOEID.

Wimmer, H. (1996) The non-word reading deficit in developmental dyslexia: evidence from children learning to read German, *Journal of Experimental Child Psychology*, 61: 80–90.

Wimmer, H., Landerl, K., Linortner, R. and Hummer, P. (1991) The relationship of phonemic awareness to reading acquisition: more consequence than precondition but still important, *Cognition*, 40: 219–49.

Wimmer, H., Landerl, K. and Schneider, W. (1994) The role of rhyme awareness in learning to read a regular orthography, *British Journal of Developmental Psychology*, 12: 469–84.

Ziegler, J.C. and Goswami, U. (2005) Reading acquisition, developmental dyslexia and skilled reading across languages: a psycholinguistic grain size theory, *Psychological Bulletin*, 131 (1): 3–29.

Ziegler, J.C. and Goswami, U. (2006) Becoming literate in different languages: similar problems, different solutions, *Developmental Science*, 9: 429–53.

Ziegler, J.C., Stone, G.O. and Jacobs, A.M. (1997). What's the pronunciation for –OUGH and the spelling for /u/? A database for computing feedforward and feedback inconsistency in English, *Behavior Research Methods, Instruments, & Computers*, 29: 600–18.

9   Inquiry into meaning: a conversation

Myra Barrs and Margaret Meek Spencer

MB   We have been rereading and talking about a long-itudinal study of learning to read that we both admire greatly and feel should be more widely read and known. The book is called *Inquiry into Meaning* and it was originally published in 1985 by Lawrence Erlbaum Associates (Bussis *et al.* 1985). A revised edition reappeared in 2001, published by Teachers' College Press (Chittenden *et al.* 2001).

MS   It was a deep disappointment when the book went out of print; it had never occurred to me that it could. Although more than 20 years have passed since this unique reading research enterprise was first pub-lished, we believe its nature and findings are still relevant to most recent studies. The revised version amply confirms my belief that this is the best book I've read about reading and the role of teachers in reading research.

MB   *Inquiry into Meaning* appeared at a point when psycholinguists like Kenneth Goodman had made a seismic difference to the study of the reading process, by articulating the ways in which readers draw on different cueing systems in order to make sense of texts. Like Mina Shaughnessy, in observing learners at work Goodman drew attention to 'the intelligence of their mistakes'. In the 1980s we were applying these insights to the teaching of literacy. At the Centre for Language in Primary Education (CLPE), where we were developing the *Primary Language*

Record for the Inner London Education Authority (ILEA), we incorporated them into the sampling procedures contained in the PLR (Barrs *et al.* 1988).

MS The editors of the revised version of the original *Inquiry* recognize their affiliation with *Primary Language Record* by including it in their account of notable developments in assessment since 1985. This kind of close observation wasn't new in 1985. In the 1970s, common understanding of children's language was being transformed when linguists and teachers collected it and scrupulously described both language and learning. Michael Halliday's transcriptions of his son's early speech appeared as *Learning How to Mean* (1975). When the *Inquiry* was in progress, so was Henrietta Dombey's study of Anna taking her first steps in 'learning the language of books', which reveals what the *Inquiry* writers distinguish as knowledge.

MB There is a strong sense throughout the book of the kindergarten, first and second grade classrooms that the teachers and children work in, a busy and optimistic buzz, and a broad picture of the whole range of their activities. These are predominantly urban schools in New York and Philadelphia and two-thirds of the children in the study are African American. Over the two years of the study, we watch most of them becoming confident and successful readers.

MS For the purposes of this article we have shared the writing. Myra introduces the original forward-looking nature of the research project with its unique emphasis on observation. She also sets out the discriminating features of the data collection and the ways devised by the researchers to record the children's modes of learning and their growth as readers. Margaret looks at the notion of learning 'styles', and then reports on two case studies, which bring together the elaborate qualitative detail of two years of classroom observations.

Myra Barrs writes:

I first read *Inquiry into Meaning* shortly after it appeared in 1985. I had just joined the CLPE and Moira McKenzie, then CLPE Director, had brought it back from the USA and passed it on to me. I spent the next few months reading it and rereading it. Initially I was puzzled by its provenance; all of its authors were members of ETS, an American organization for educational testing. But when I discussed the book with James Britton he referred me to a previous title by the same team, *Beyond Surface Curriculum*, one of his favourite books of classroom-based research (Bussis *et al.* 1976). Like *Inquiry into Meaning*, this book based its findings on observations taken from the daily life of the classroom.

In this respect, as in others, *Inquiry into Meaning* was like no other book about learning to read that I had ever come across. As a six-year study with two three-year cycles, containing two successive longitudinal studies of children in their first two years of school, it was shapely in its design and impressive in its planning. But the most astonishing thing about it was its basis in systematic observation of children (and teachers) in classrooms, and the quality of this observation, which depended on close collaboration between teachers and researchers. Out of this came a research report which at times read like a novel, so vivid and individual were its portraits of young literacy learners.

The researchers were not reading specialists, and perhaps because of this they came to the subject with fresh eyes. They were less interested in testing out theories of reading than in finding out what readers did – this is a book about readers, not about reading. They were also not concerned so much to generalize about readers' behaviour, as to look squarely at the differences between them and at the individual styles and approaches that they brought to beginning to read. And they wanted to study children's learning of reading in the context of their learning as a whole.

So here was a book about learning to read that regarded children's drawings and paintings, their modelling and construction, their use of maths materials, their sewing, their dramatic play, as relevant to a study of children learning literacy. In addition, the observers paid close attention to children's interactions with teachers, with other adults in the classroom, and with each other, resulting in an intensely social and authentic picture of what learning looks like.

Everything that I found in *Inquiry into Meaning* about how children make sense of learning to read, and how they bring themselves to that learning, fitted right in with all the discussions about learning that I had taken part in at the London Institute of Education, with James Britton and other teachers. It drew, as Britton so frequently did, on the work of George Kelly and on his psychology of personal constructs, which looked at the way in which individuals interpret the world according to their experience. The 'interpretative structure' which children brought to their learning was what the research team sought to define in their analysis of individual case studies.

In addition, Kelly's emphasis on systematic observation and documentation as the means of 'understanding others' understandings' resonated strongly with the work that many of us in the London Association of the Teachers of English (LATE) and elsewhere had been doing on classroom observation. I had edited Michael Armstrong's *Closely Observed Children* (1980) for Writers and Readers, and there was much in his way of taking a broad look at children's learning over time that chimed with the approach of *Inquiry into Meaning*.

A constant companion

Over the years that followed I went on reading and rereading *Inquiry into Meaning*. Although initially I had read it mainly for its view of learning to read, in subsequent readings I focused more closely on what it had to teach me about conducting educational research – how to tame the mass of messy data that observation in classrooms often produces. I was beginning the long haul of doing a part-time PhD and my research design was heavily influenced by *Inquiry into Meaning*. What I liked about it was its combination of naturalistic observation, fine description and rigour in interpreting and analysing data.

From then on, this book was to become my constant companion in a series of research studies which CLPE undertook into different aspects of literacy, culminating in the studies published as *The Reader in the Writer* (Barrs and Cork 2001) and *Boys on the Margin* (Safford et al. 2004). Both studies were grounded in case study, and in both cases the CLPE research team set out to follow individual children over a period of several months, working closely with their teachers. We took other features from *Inquiry into Meaning* too, including the use of 'standard' texts, ones that were common to all the classrooms being observed. This enabled us to make valuable generalizations about what different children took from these texts in very varying contexts.

The theory

In the first edition, as in this new edition, the book falls into two halves, with the researchers setting out the research model and its theoretical outcomes in the first half and the case studies in the second half. This means that by the time you come to the case studies (only three in this edition, rather than the original four) you are able to read them through the researchers' eyes, and find in them evidence for their theory.

The first half, though dense, is intensely rewarding. It is both thorough in its approach and yet also concise in its statements. Its conception of reading is as an example of skill learning, in which children have to bring together several different kinds of knowledge in the *act* of reading. The team express their view of the process in the following economical definition in which every word counts:

> *Reading is the act of orchestrating diverse knowledge in order to construct meaning from text while maintaining reasonable fluency and reasonable accountability to the information contained in the writing.*

> (Chittenden *et al.* 2001: 40, original italics)

The accompanying diagram (Figure 9.1) shows a triangle, of which the apex is meaning, the goal of the whole process. The base of the triangle is the 'diverse knowledge' (e.g. knowledge of book content, syntactic knowledge, phonetic knowledge) that readers bring to reading – sometimes called 'cueing systems'. The sides of the triangle are the two aspects of the act that have to work together: anticipation (fluency) and accountability to the words on the page (accuracy). The definition concludes: 'The act begins when the knowledge is orchestrated.' (p. 41)

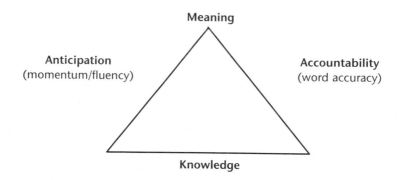

Figure 9.1: Schematic conception of reading
Source: Chittenden *et al.* 2001

It was this concept of 'orchestration' that was so immensely helpful to me in thinking about what readers do. By viewing reading as an example of skill learning, the team showed that the key for the learner was to be able to put everything together in real time. They gave a convincing explanation of how it is that readers 'learn to read by reading':

> The paradox of skill learning is that novices can begin to practise before they control all the requisite knowledge that enters a polished performance ... As long as a person possesses some of the necessary knowledge and understands what the skill is intended to accomplish, practice can start. And once started, the brain picks up additional knowledge in the course of practice efforts.
>
> Chittenden *et al.* 2001: 41)

It was through their understanding of how learning happens, and how the brain strives to make meaning, and through their ability to apply these understandings to the thorny subject of beginning reading, that these researchers were able to present a commonsensical and satisfying view of what Huey called 'the most remarkable specific performance ...'.

Knowledge resources

The chapter on the different kinds of knowledge that underpin learning to read is one of my favourites. The chapter is full of illuminating examples of children using what they know to try to make sense of texts. They can be detracked when their expectations – their logical, linguistic, or syntactic expectations – are violated. Crystal initially refuses to read 'A blue dog on a red tree. A red dog on a blue tree' because she thinks that logically the blue dog should be on the blue tree (p. 45). When children meet unfamiliar syntactic structures their reading may falter, but what this shows, as the authors point out, is their great sensitivity to grammatical structures.

The researchers point out that all the children in the study began reading with two strong knowledge resources at their disposal: enough background knowledge to understand the content of many books, and a firm grasp of the syntactic structures and sound patterns of English. The majority of them also had knowledge of sound–letter relationships and most had received systematic instruction in phonics. 'But the bulk of the additional knowledge they acquired *about* reading, they acquired *by* reading' (p. 70). This included knowledge that nobody thought fit to tell them about anyway, such as knowledge of spelling patterns and knowledge of stylistic differences between different authors or genres. Yet children learned these differences and their knowledge helped them to read better.

Two examples from this chapter stand out for me. One is from the section on 'Background knowledge of book content', which shows how much knowledge of the world children bring to their reading. It concerns the reading of *Blackboard Bear*, one of the 'standard texts' read by all the children (Alexander 1969). This attractive book, with its themes of loneliness, bullying, rejection and retribution, appealed to all the children. They recognized its undertones and 'their grasp of the material seemed to develop as they went along' (p. 47). The study team noted that all of the less proficient readers read this text with greater fluency than was typical of them; these readers recognized and were helped by their knowledge of the human situation in the text. It seems that the book was an example of one of those 'emotionally powerful' texts that the CLPE research published as *The Reader in the Writer* found to be particularly helpful to children learning to write.

The section of the chapter entitled 'Knowledge of literary styles and rhythms' is in itself a significant contribution to the literature on beginning reading. It looks at children's quasi-reading and the way in which they seem to commit to memory:

> ... the phrase structures of a story. The individual words flowed from the structures. That is, children encode stories in memory not as individual word pieces but as segmented, rhythmic sequences.
>
> (Chittenden *et al.* 2001: 55)

Children's sensitivity to literary structures, and to rhyme, and how this supports their reading, is beautifully exemplified in this section. As the researchers point out, there is a paradox in the fact that 'more artful forms of writing' are ostensibly harder for beginning readers to negotiate, but may actually be easier to anticipate than 'the choppy stilted prose typical of so many books for beginners'. Basal readers which are 'designed to foster analytic knowledge of letter–sound relationships' lack language flow and rhythm; they concentrate attention only on accuracy, thus actually impeding fluency in reading.

For a book investigating learning to read, *Inquiry into Meaning* spends remarkably little time on a discussion of phonic knowledge, but what it does have to say about the 'phonetic information contained in the writing' is of absorbing interest. The researchers are, of course, interested both in children's *implicit* and their *explicit* knowledge of letter–sound relationships. Their implicit knowledge was revealed by their substitutions, or miscues; when reading, children would often substitute a word that matched the text word in two or more 'phonemic segments' (e.g. **pat** for **pet**, **care** for **core**). The researchers noted that although most children were obviously drawing on letter–sound knowledge, 'For some, only a portion of their working knowledge could be formalized in words.'

Many children's phonic knowledge came from direct teaching; over half were in classrooms where there was a systematic phonics programme and most of these, in their workbook exercises, showed explicit knowledge of phonic rules. But they could not always use this knowledge easily in their reading. For instance: 'Only about 20 per cent were able to analyse and synthesize sounds in a conscious blending strategy with reasonably consistent accuracy.' Sometimes children failed to recognize the very words that they had conscientiously sounded out – words such as **definitely**, for example. Sometimes they found phonic rules unreliable – as when Crystal tried to read **pu**t but found that its 'u' sound was different from that in words like **but**, **cut**, or **hut**.

Children's records showed that even children who were 'adept at phonic analysis' didn't operate solely on the basis of phonic rules in their reading, and that for most children 'the blending of sound segments was simply not a workable strategy'. Their reading was based on several different kinds of knowledge, and their learning to read was a matter of learning to draw on all these sources of information in the act of reading. But they went about this very differently, and these differences were linked to other aspects of their learning.

Orchestration

The researchers underline the fact that children were more alike in *what* they knew about reading and print than in *how* they used this knowledge in reading. The diversity of ways in which they went about this complex task revealed the importance of individual styles in learning and it also brought out the key role of orchestration in skill learning. The researchers understand the demands that young learners face when they are learning to juggle, or orchestrate, multiple resources. 'The orchestration of knowledge' is the chapter that makes *Inquiry into Meaning* into such a key text for understanding literacy learning.

In this chapter, the researchers summarize the results of a series of 'detailed procedures' that they devised for analysing children's oral reading of the 'standard texts'. The results of these analyses allowed them to make some generalizations about how children used what they knew about reading and books when they approached an unknown text. The 'procedures' they devised were ingenious ways of focusing on different aspects of the orchestration process.

For instance, through a 'control index' they found that the children all showed increasing control as they read through a book. The researchers looked at how readers read the second half of the book compared with the first half, and sometimes found dramatic increases in control in the second half of the book. This evidence led them to stress that 'a capacity to build on growing familiarity with the material' is apparent when children read whole texts. It's a nice proof of what we may feel we know about the role of the text in reading – the way that a text can support a reader – and it's also important evidence of the value of assessing reading in the context of reading whole texts.

They also showed, through an adaptation of miscue analysis, that children approached a basal reader differently from the way in which they read a trade book (*Big Dog, Little Dog*). Readers varied their strategies, relying more on grammatical cues in reading the trade book, and more on letter–sound knowledge in reading the basal reader. They were clearly attending to the way the texts were written, adapting their reading styles to the books' writing styles. In the course of reading both books children's miscues got 'better', more responsive to a wider range of cues. But the exercise had shown, as the authors say, that beginning readers 'make adaptive adjustments to text variation in much the same manner as mature readers' (p. 89). (And it had also shown that books constructed primarily to give children practice in phonic decoding don't enable them to draw on a full range of cues.)

The third coding procedure is at the core of the book's view that children exhibit very different styles as readers from the beginning, and that these are related to their overall learning styles. In this procedure, the researchers looked at the relationship between momentum and accuracy in children's reading, by tracking their 'unmodified' and 'modified' (or self-corrected) deviations (errors) in reading selected texts over a period of two years. This procedure revealed that two-thirds of the children showed a decided preference *either* for maintaining momentum (fluency) *or* for upholding accuracy *from the outset*. Over the course of the two years, most of these children achieved 'an increasing balance between momentum and accuracy'.

In order to do this, some readers who favoured momentum over accuracy (like Carrie, who always 'plunged into reading' confidently, ad-libbing where necessary) had to slow down and self-correct more. Others (like Rita, who from the start was preoccupied with accuracy and read slowly, losing a sense of the overall meaning) had to quicken up and make more unmodified errors, self-correcting less. Graphs (see Figure 9.2) give clear evidence of this convergence happening between these two children early in the second year of schooling.

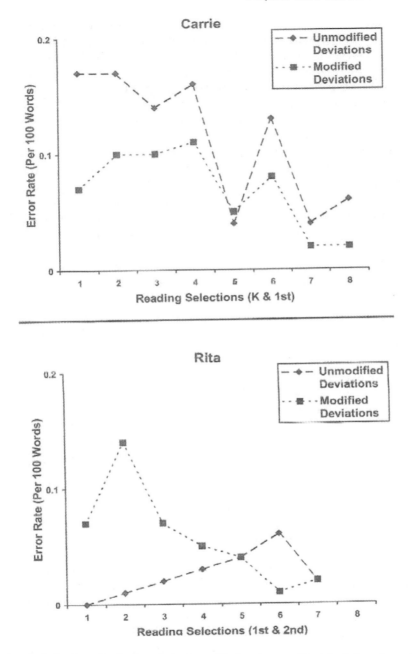

Figure 9.2: Longitudinal analysis of modified and unmodified deviations in reading selections spanning two school years
Source: Chittenden *et al.* 2001: 93

As they achieved more balance, both became more effective readers, and so did all the children with similarly strong initial preferences.

Analysis of observations and samples

These 'detailed proceedings' and 'codings' for looking at reading behaviour emerged from the wider study of individual children's reading over two years, which was the foundation of the individual 'child studies'. The findings on children's stylistic preferences in reading were derived not just from reading assessments, but from a thorough analysis of children's overall patterns of learning in the classroom. The researchers hypothesized that these readers' different stylistic approaches were expressing something quite fundamental about them as learners.

In charting children's individual patterns of learning, the researchers used an unusual approach to analysis. They drew on classroom observation, teachers' records, work samples (including photographs of art and construction work) and oral reading samples. They modelled their methodology on the work of Patricia Carini, of the Prospect Centre in Philadelphia who, working with teachers, had developed data analysis and integration processes to identify themes and patterns in children's learning.

This data analysis work was done by small teams: the teacher and two researchers who knew the child well, and three other collaborators who did not know the child. It involved a thorough chronological review of children's records, work samples and reading samples over two years. The team looked for patterns in the data, and created sets of descriptive headings to describe these patterns. The headings were tested out by trawling through the data again, and then revised and adapted. The authors say that initially headings are 'tantamount to impressions' but, once interrogated more thoroughly, they become 'considered interpretations'. In addition, the teams undertook what were termed 'descriptive analyses' of samples of children's work. These procedures were carried out methodically, and repeated to make sure that the patterns that were emerging would stand up to scrutiny. All of this, of course, very much recalls the approaches described by Glaser and Strauss in *The Discovery of Grounded Theory*, although this influential text is not mentioned in the bibliography.

The quality of the researchers' observations and their responsiveness to children's meanings and intentions make this an unusually rich book. The child studies, with their anecdotes, transcripts, photographs and observations of reading, are structured around the researchers' headings.

For instance, the case study of Crystal links her self-set standards and sense of quality in sewing (she will pull all the stitches out of a purse if she's not satisfied with what she's done) with the care and persistence that she brings to literacy activities.

Since the publication of *Inquiry into Meaning*, with the growth of ethnographically based research, we have had many more studies of classrooms which bring learning to life and derive theory from detailed studies of learners. But it's the combination of scrupulous, detailed and thoughtful attention to observational data from classrooms and elegantly designed small-scale quantitative studies which makes this a one-off book. Although the authors bring enormous experience to the research design, it's their open-mindedness that makes this work so special. Their conclusions do truly emerge from the data, and they have a reach and a significance which means that they still have something to say to us today. As a study of beginning reading it's a remarkably refreshing and sane contribution to the literature; there are no noises here of axes being ground.

This is also that rare thing, a true longitudinal study, showing us learners' individual journeys as they move into reading. Whenever I have occasion to discuss either reading or research methodology with anybody, I always end up talking about *Inquiry into Meaning*.

Margaret Meek Spencer writes:

I have no accurate recollection of how I came to read *Inquiry into Meaning*. Searching for clues, I found the publication details in my ordinary diary for 1986, but there were no further references to the book or its contents in the work files and notebooks of that period. Most likely, the prompt to buy it (instead of using the library copy) came from the reading company I kept then at the Institute of Education, the London Association for the Teaching of English, and CLPE. The effect of reading it: amazement, deep, serious admiration for its scope and analytic detail, relief, and some envy, has accompanied my every return to its contents.

It isn't a book about failure, reading method or materials: nor is it about adults, who know about reading, teaching children who don't. Instead, as Deborah Meier says in the first line of the new text, 'this book describes one of those rare efforts to see what children do, in their own terms, when they take on the challenge of something complex, like learning to read'(Chittenden *et al.* 2001: ix). Here, the children enlighten their teachers who in turn observe, explore and interpret, with great subtlety, the complex nature of the evidence that becomes available.

Patterns of learning

The central tenet of the *Inquiry* is that all children have unique patterns of learning, which characterize their individuality. Teachers in classrooms know these personal styles as differences between children who seem to have other things in common: age, developmental stage, local culture, range of abilities, and yet are distinctive as learners. Having established the nature of children's orchestration of the knowledge they bring to school learning, the writers confirm that most children display a 'decisive preference' for attending to either the momentum or the accuracy aspects of reading aloud. That is, they see learning to read either as a necessity to keep going through the text, or as an obligation to give an exact rendition of the words on the page. When (as the first edition of the book says) 'the going got rough', the preferred moves made by the children when they read were seen as part of their personal learning styles, which they exhibited in other classroom activities.

The researchers distinguish these stylistic preferences from knowledge. They clearly influence children's learning, including their learning to read, in ways that can be described, but they have rarely, if ever, appeared in research inquiries. Figure 9.3 is a summary of styles the writers identify as part of general classroom activities. The differences between them relate to the *meanings* the children choose to demonstrate. The authors claim that children's early style preferences seem to extend into later behaviour as judgements about how best to make sense of the world.

Style	Cluster A	Cluster B
Preferred expressions of meaning	Imaginative and divergent	Realistic and convergent
Manner of work	Mobile and fluid	Contained and methodical
Additional scope and emphasis	Broad and integrative	Narrowed and analytic
Sequence of thought	Parallel sequencing	Linear sequencing

Figure 9.3:
Source: Chittenden *et al.* 2001: 98

In their discussions of stylistic influences in learning, the writers selected their contrasting evidence from a wide range of classroom activities. Some children drew realistic pictures; others experimented more fancifully with different materials and media. Some enjoyed the 'mess of clay, paint and paste', others tidied their activities away. Some moved freely through the space of the classroom, in contrast to those who delineated their workspace and stayed within it. Again, the emphasis is on the range and variety of children's preferences when they have the chance to choose. But it was the 'active nature of reading' which supplied the details for the momentum and accuracy distinction related to the orchestration of knowledge. These same details also revealed the relevance of styles to learning how to read. The contrasting evidence comes from the children in the clusters A and B in the summary above (Figure 9.3).

Cluster A includes children who put their energy into maintaining their oral reading momentum to gather up meaning. They press on, dealing with their miscues en route. When they encounter unknown or difficult words and phrases, a characteristic move is to repeat the easy, known words so as to gain time for the next attack on the difficulty. In their quasi-reading, Jenny and Carrie had a range of tactics: they role-played reading, speaking aloud in a book-reading voice, skipping words, inventing others. Faced with uncertainty, they guessed and kept going, a process that lasted until their performances began to show a greater concern for fidelity to the text. When Debbie began to negotiate text, she 'used several tactics to sustain momentum. She omitted, she repeated, she substituted, she relied on her intuitive sense of rhythm and she refused to fuss or worry about mistakes' (p. 127). Jack skipped along sentences, reading ahead to sort out the words. He then approximated the words and moved on. Tim juxtaposed words and sometimes read two words at a time; both are indicators of keeping up momentum, as is his 'gliding from one activity to another' (p. 105).

Cluster B is the accuracy group. They attended to every word, pausing at some length until they 'worked something out' and rarely read ahead. Like Louis, they were aware of the constraint of rules. Dana would not read anything until he had practised it. His preferred expressions of meanings were consistently realistic; his thinking convergent, especially in his drawings. He stuck to the rules for carrying out tasks 'to the bitter end', even when it was not necessary to do so.

These are the briefest glimpses into the characteristic styles of how the children expressed meaning as they began to learn to read. In both groups the children had stylistic tendencies in common, but this did not mean that they were identical. Later, when they were confronted with more difficult texts in the operational phase of the research, these initial approaches to reading returned. The practical implications suggested are to let children rely 'in a large part on their stylistic strengths. Or, to state the principle conversely, don't cut them off from the seat of their best judgement'. In busy classrooms, teachers need assistants who can help to raise awareness of these particular kinds of discernment.

Child studies

Reading the details of the period when the children were closely observed and documented, I felt I was coming to know them. There is no doubt that they are the lively elements in the *Inquiry*. Right at the beginning, once the research context is settled, the reader meets Dana and Jenny in Ms Lichert's classroom. Details from the lives of Colin, Debbie, Jack, Meg, Tanya, Rita and others provide data relevant to each child's reading style and its 'theoretic formulation'. As child studies they are presented in a 'standard format' which brings together a synopsis – a sketch of each child's learning patterns and progress; the Instructional Environment and Reading Program – what happens in school; a Report from the Total Record and a Report from the Reading Record. There are subsections in each of these, and also dialogues with other children, contrasts of reality and imagination, descriptions of contexts, sideways glances at children's book reading, all in thick descriptions that extend our awareness of reading as learning. Here are two of them, Louis and Carrie, representative respectively of Cluster B and Cluster A (p. 98).

Louis

In school contexts where accuracy, obeying rules and paying attention are expected from pupils, Louis might have been an ideal pupil. These characteristics form an important part of his learning styles. He also has the affective resources of patience, exactness, purposefulness, constancy and willpower, combined with a steady interest in what he is doing, especially when he is working with modular materials such as Lego. He does what he is told. His attachment to realism in his drawing and use of materials confirms him as a typical member of the B cluster. Anxious to be correct at all times in behaviour as in meaning making, he tends to keep home and school apart. Although these aspects suggest forms of repression, there is also evidence that Louis benefits from his meticulous singularities. For example, he knows a lot about rules and how to apply them: they are useful knowledge in tests. By successful elaboration of what he does bit by bit, he works like an expert. His model Lego service station is both artful in design and representative of his making things that do things. Books of information, especially those with pictures, are his preferred texts.

One of the undoubted benefits of the close study over time is that change is expected. Later, the observers recorded certain unexpected, affective qualities: an inclination toward fantasy and inner imaginative thinking. From time to time Louis told jokes. The remaining problem was that, while he understood what the concept of reading was, why books were important and how sequencing was involved, he could not bring himself to read a text aloud. He never guessed words, nor did he risk saying them in case he made mistakes. In ways the careful recordings make plain he became less afraid of the unexpected. But, on the whole, it was difficult for him to give up his 'tracking' systems and his habit of treating words as discrete units. Unfamiliar texts were always a trial. His writing showed comparable difficulties. In both reading and writing he wanted to create a text that makes the kind of sense he knew about, but his way with words, treating them as single entities, inhibited his understanding. The writers suggest that:

> One source of difficulty may be the way memory is developed during oral reading, in contrast with its role in the construction process Louis excels in. In the case of assembling and fitting together units of a concrete material such as Lego, the material itself provides a running record of the history of the structure. The work in process is constantly available, effectively eliminating the need for a memory trace in the mind of the builder. In reading, however, given the perishable nature of the spoken word and the limitations of short-term memory, no concrete residue of the textual meaning remains. Unless reading proceeds apace and the reader uses the variety of mnemonic devices available to fix meaning – such as repetition, self-correction, and summarizing, meaning will not be retained.
>
> (Chittenden *et al.* 2001: 241).

Louis's early insistence on reading word by word meant that his oral reading was devoid of meaning. The slow movement of his learning to write, moving towards making his own meanings, concludes his case study on a more optimistic note. For me this kind of insight is an example of why this book is so important.

Carrie

Carrie is the most confident and successful reader in the book. Her presence seeps into other chapters where she appears by way of example or contrast. Out of curiosity I counted the number of pages where she appears – 51 in all. Everything recorded about her is directly relevant to the concerns of the *Inquiry*. She brings to it the personality of a small, vivid African American, charged with confidence, skill, affectivity, imagination and independence, in a full-day kindergarten in New York.

She is a reader from the start.

The rhetorical question the writers ask is: how does she 'smoothly' acquire a working knowledge of print without abandoning her adherence to story and her confidence that she is a reader of stories (p.144)? The answer begins with evidence of how she balances momentum and accuracy by adopting the role of a narrator. This means she can keep the story in place, while planning ahead and still paying attention to the telling. It's the best example of parallel sequencing in these child studies. There is no direct evidence of where her storying originates, but school provides a rich repertoire and much encouragement. I was intrigued by the mention of Breakthrough Books, and the writing-oriented materials from the same source, as part of the school's equipment for teaching literacy. Traces of Carrie's reading appear in her writing. Experiences of literary sequences and rhythms in stories read to her are reflected in the tales she tells. An emphasis on dramatic play and performance is stronger here than anywhere else.

Three things stand out: first, her keen sense of an audience. She knows what it is to be an engaged listener and expects the same attention from those to whom she artfully tells her own tales. Sometimes her hearers are over-convinced of her veracity. Next, we see her interrogating a text: how can a bear in a book come alive? As for doing things smoothly, she diversifies her practice by seeking out books of different kinds. For me, her strongest understanding about reading is that the reader has to become both the teller and the told. Her teacher encourages the children to think about what they are doing. Carrie is apt to do this aloud so that we can follow her train of thought. Experience of literary sequences and rhythms in stories read to her are again reflected in the tales she tells.

As she pays more attention to print she seems to realize that what she says and what she sees on the page have a matching relationship and so begins to feel some obligation to the text to get it right. The way Carrie tunes into the patterns and cadences of texts shows how firm is her engagement in learning to read. In addition, there are interesting references to the part that memory seems to play in Carrie's recursive practices. These kinds of evidence are outside or beyond commonly used measurements of reading competences. They also offer encouragement to those who believe that literacy and literature should be more closely linked in research. For all our various formal and informal preoccupations with reviving the teaching of reading in school, the child studies and constant exemplification from the work of other children in the project throw into relief our lack of current evidence of how children actually go about learning to do it.

MB   Since 1985 the world of reading has changed greatly.
          What kind of a reading scene does this book enter
          now?

MS   It's a world where the question of how reading
          should be taught has become ever more politicized.
          In the past two years we've seen a Select Committee
          of the House of Commons (2005) investigating
          reading teaching methods and recommending a
          review of the National Literacy Strategy, as well as
          'large-scale, comparative research on the best ways
          of teaching children to read, comparing synthetic
          phonics "fast and first" with other methods'. The
          summary of the Committee's findings makes it quite
          clear that they came to favour a greater emphasis on
          synthetic phonics in the initial teaching of reading
          and that they essentially accepted the criticisms that
          they had received of the National Literacy Strategy
          from a number of sources, including the Reading
          Reform Foundation and Ruth Miskin of ReadWrite
          Inc.

MB   That Select Committee Report was followed by the
          one-man investigation into the teaching of early
          reading by Jim Rose which, predictably, came to the
          conclusion that:

> there is much convincing evidence to show from
> the practice observed that, as generally under-
> stood, 'synthetic' phonics is the form of systematic
> phonic work that offers the vast majority of
> beginners the best route to becoming skilled
> readers. Among other strengths, this is because it
> teaches children directly what they need to know
> ...whereas other approaches, such as 'analytic'
> phonics, expect children to deduce them.
>
> (Rose 2006: 19)

          It does seem curious, doesn't it, that approaches
          which teach children to think, and which engage
          them in active learning, are here implicitly down-
          graded.

MS   Yes, and nobody in this debate appears to be paying
          nearly enough attention to the main finding of
          Inquiry into Meaning: that it's what children *do* with
          what they're taught that is interesting – and that they

respond very differently to their teaching.

Rose's report put too much credence on the Clackmannanshire study (2005) by Johnston and Watson, which compared the progress of a group of children being taught by a synthetic phonics programme with that of a control group. There have been several thoughtful critics of Johnston and Watson, chief among whom is Usha Goswami, who maintain that this study has basic flaws. But it came along at a point when policy makers needed a 'scientific' study to support what one can only see as a political decision to give government backing to synthetic phonics as the royal road to reading.

MB The Reading Reform Foundation duly gave a warm welcome to the Rose Review. It had delivered what no other government report had yet provided – an endorsement of the case that the RRF had been making for several years, at least since the introduction of the National Curriculum. This has been a most effective lobbying group, initially supported by a parallel organization in the USA which succeeded in getting phonics into the political programme of the Republican Party. There's no question that lobby groups such as the Reading Reform Foundation and the Dyslexia Association have had a disproportionate amount of influence on government educational policies, and that their systematic lobbying has paid off. Ken Goodman has a very clear account of this process in the United States in a chapter called 'The politics of phonics' in his book *Phonic Phacts* (1993).

MS All of this has resulted in what the DfES calls the 'new conceptual framework' for teaching reading: 'The Simple View of Reading'. The relatively complex 'searchlights model' of reading in the NLS, which at least acknowledged something of the complexity of learning to read and the reading process, is now being boiled down into a model with only two components: word recognition and language comprehension. Against this we might set *Inquiry into Meaning*'s description of reading as 'a complex but singular skill' and their caution that 'the greater the level of skill complexity, the more resources (knowledge and capabilities) enter the act'.

MB   As part of this general trend towards simplification there's a definite movement, again promoted by the Reading Reform Foundation, to use 'decodable reading books in the early stages of learning to read'. The Rose Review says there's 'some force' to the view that decodable texts might help children to practise their phonic skills and achieve early success. We must hope that we don't find educational policy going too far down that road, which would cut the youngest children off from one of the main satisfactions of reading, the pleasure of the text.

MS   The problem is that far too few people involved in research into literacy are sufficiently interested in the content of reading – in *what* is being read, and in *how* that affects children's learning to read. *Inquiry into Meaning* shows us clearly how these children's reading changed and grew in response to texts which were emotionally engaging, or to books with marked literary styles and rhythms. This is important evidence, and it's why I think the book might offer the beginning of a different tradition, one that didn't consist of either/or, that didn't accept a separation of literacy from literature, but that brought these diverse traditions together and integrated them.

MB   Unfortunately that looks quite unlikely at present. What works against it is the current government emphasis on 'evidence-based practice', which is the real reason why the phonics lobby have been so successful in their attempts to put phonics at the centre of reading instruction this time around. Research that conforms to the standards laid down by the UK's Evidence for Policy and Practice Information Centre (EPPI-Centre), or to the US's What Works Clearinghouse, is based on traditional scientific paradigms: it deals in studies which employ comparison or control groups, which use pre- and post-testing, which result in statistically significant findings, and so on. While this kind of limited paradigm dictates what counts as evidence, and while this kind of evidence influences policy, a study like *Inquiry into Meaning* will never achieve the much wider recognition that it deserves. The researchers provide a wealth of qualitative data, all underpinned by scrupulous data analysis and those elegant small-scale quantitative studies. It's powerful stuff, but does academic research in reading recognize this as evidence?

MS   Nevertheless, our contention is that this book makes qualitative evidence important on anyone's terms, and that ignoring it calls all the rest into question. It's no real good delving into discrete bits of the process in the way that the studies Rose cites do; you need to see the task from the point of view of the learner and understand all that's influencing their learning. *Inquiry into Meaning* shows us clearly that this is not only all the aspects of reading that we've touched on here but also the individual reader's disposition towards the process, and the teacher's need to recognize that and respond to it. By putting children's meaning making at the heart of their learning to read, *Inquiry into Meaning* becomes a critique of official ways of assessing learning at this time.

References

Alexander, M. (1969) *Blackboard Bear*. New York: Dial Press.

Armstrong, M. (1980) *Closely Observed Children*. London. Writers and Readers Publishing Cooperative.

Barrs, M. (1995) Imagination in Action. Unpublished PhD thesis.

Barrs, M. and Cork, V. (2001) *The Reader in the Writer: The Links between the Study of Literature and Writing Development at Key Stage 2*. London: Centre for Literacy in Primary Education.

Barrs, M., Ellis, S., Hester, H. and Thomas, A. (1988) *Primary Language Record*. London: CLPE.

Britton, J.N. (1970) *Language and Learning*. Harmondsworth: Penguin.

Bussis, A., Chittenden, E. and Amarel, M. (1976) *Beyond Surface Curriculum*. Boulder, CO.: Westview Press.

Bussis, A.M., Chittenden, E.A., Amarel, M. and Klausner, E. (1985) *Inquiry into Meaning: An Investigation of Learning to Read*. Hillsdale, NJ: Lawrence Erlbaum Associates.

Carini, P.F. (1975) *Observation and Description: An Alternative Methodology for the Investigation of Human Phenomena*. Monograph of the North Dakota Study Group on Evaluation. Grand Forks, ND: University of Dakota Press.

Chittenden, E. and Salinger, T., with Bussis, A.M. (2001) *Inquiry into Meaning: An Investigation of Learning to Read,* revised edition, with an introduction by Deborah Meier. New York and London: Teachers College Press.

Dombey, H. (1983) 'Learning the language of books' in M. Meek *et al. Opening Moves: Work in Progress in the Study of Children's Language Development*. Bedford Way Paper 17. London: Institute of Education.

Eastman, P.D. (1969) *Big Dog ... Little Dog: A Bedtime Story*. London: Random House.

Glaser, B.G. and Strauss, A.L. (1967) *The Discovery of Grounded Theory: Strategies for Qualitative Research*. Chicago, IL: Aldine.

Goodman, K. (1993) *Phonic Phacts*. Scholastic Canada: Ontario.

Halliday, M.A.K. (1975) *Learning How to Mean*. London: Edward Arnold.

House of Commons Education and Skills Committee (2005) *Teaching Children to Read: Eighth Report of Session 2004–05*. London: House of Commons.

Huey, E.B. (1908 [1968]) *The Psychology and Pedagogy of Reading, with a Review of the History of Reading and Writing and of Methods, Texts and Hygiene in Reading*. Cambridge MA: MIT.

Johnston, R. and Watson, J. (2005) *The Effects of Synthetic Phonics Teaching on Reading and Spelling Attainment*. Edinburgh: Scottish Executive Education Department.

Kelly, G.A.D. (1955) *A Theory of Personal Constructs, Vol. 1: A Theory of Personality*. New York: W.W. Norton & Co.

Mackay, D., Thompson, B. and Schaub, P. (1970) *Breakthrough to Literacy*. London: Longman.

Rose, J. (2006) *An Independent Review of the Teaching of Early Reading*. Nottingham: DfES

Safford, K., O'Sullivan, O. and Barrs, M. (2004) *Boys on the Margin: Promoting Boys' Literacy at Key Stage 2*. London: CLPE.

Shaughnessy, M. (1977) *Errors and Expectations*. New York: Oxford University Press.

10 Revisiting reading for pleasure: diversity, delight and desire

Teresa Cremin

Reading can change your life, it can inform, motivate, inspire and elevate; but it must be reading you do for yourself, at your own pace, in your own way, and that has a bearing on your own background, interests, values, beliefs and aspirations. Reading that is forced on you in a mechanistic way and formally assessed may have the reverse effect, the major purpose becoming pleasing the teacher and passing tests, and a preoccupation with form rather than substance.

(Woods 2001: 74–5)

To what extent do children in the early twenty-first century choose to read for pleasure, for leisure and for enjoyment? Are they reading for themselves, or for their teachers and the assessment system? Does the desire to read independently, to engage with others' worlds, to wonder and ponder and find out more about issues of interest run deep enough to sustain the young as readers of today and tomorrow?

In the light of findings which suggest there is a decline in reading for enjoyment, particularly among boys and children from the lowest socio-economic groups, this chapter revisits the significance of reading for pleasure. It reconsiders the value of the 'free will' reading of a range of texts, examines evidence of a decline, and underlines the importance of parents, carers and educators developing children's motivation, their delight in reading and desire to read. It also reflects upon why children choose to read, and provides vignettes of reading encounters which, in different contexts, reveal some learners' personal and social reasons for reading and sources of pleasure. Diversity in terms of texts as well as contexts is acknowledged and the principles of creative classroom practice are considered. It is argued that the profession needs to pay more attention to children's attitudes, their preferences, pleasures and perceptions of themselves as readers in order to help ensure that they develop as readers who not only can, but do chose to read, for pleasure and for life.

Potential benefits

The influence of reading achievement on academic attainment is widely recognized, for example the Programme for International Student Assessment (PISA) study shows that reading has an influence on academic attainment across the curriculum and can mitigate the effects of socio-economic status (Topping *et al.* 2003). The Progress in International Reading Literacy Study (PIRLS) also shows that being a frequent reader is more of an advantage than having well-educated parents (Mullis *et al.* 2003; Twist *et al.* 2003). Although relatively fewer studies focus on reading for pleasure, research in this area points to personal and academic benefits, including improved general knowledge (Cunningham and Stanovich 1998) and increased reading and writing ability (Krashen 1993). Reading amount and achievement have also been shown to be reciprocally related to one another (Cunningham and Stanovich 1998). Some studies highlight specific benefits including increased self-confidence as a reader (Guthrie and Alvermann 1999), a richer vocabulary, an improved capacity for comprehension (Cunningham and Stanovich 1998; Cox and Guthrie 2001) and greater pleasure in reading in later life (Aarnoutse and Van Leeuwe 1998). Reading for pleasure is also seen to be positively correlated with positive attitudes to reading (Guthrie and Alvermann 1999). As Sanacore observes, quoted in a review of reading for pleasure (Clark and Rumbold 2006), when individuals read for pleasure frequently, they

> experience the value of reading for efferent and aesthetic processes. Thus, they are more likely to read with a sense of purpose, which further supports their developing reading habit.
> (Clark and Rumbold 2006: 68)

A decline in pleasure?

However, international research evidence from PIRLS shows that whilst children in England are among the most able in the world in terms of reading achievement, they have a much poorer attitude to reading and read less often for pleasure than pupils in other countries (Mullis *et al.* 2003; Twist *et al.* 2003). Specifically, this study, which involved comparing 10-year-olds in 35 countries, ranked English children's attainment third (after Sweden and the Netherlands), but revealed that 13 per cent disliked reading compared to 6 per cent on average. When asked how confident they were about reading, only 30 per cent of the English children rated themselves as highly confident compared to an international average of 40 per cent.

The PISA Study (OECD 2002), focusing on older readers (15-year-olds), also revealed that despite high average scores in term of attainment, nearly 30 per cent of the English students never or hardly ever read for pleasure, 19 per cent felt it was a waste of time and 35 per cent said they would only read if they had to. Regardless of ability, girls were much more likely to read for pleasure than boys. In the National Literacy Trust (NLT) survey (Clark and Foster 2005), in which the views of over 8000 primary and secondary pupils were collected, overall secondary pupils and boys were more inclined to report negative attitudes than primary learners and girls. On balance this survey, which encompassed a very wide range of texts (both screen-based and on paper), suggested rather more positive attitudes to reading than those reported in the PIRLS study, although this may have been a product of the schools' involvement in Reading Connects. A decline in reading for pleasure is also reported in comparative work by Sainsbury and Schagen (2004), who collected children's attitudes to reading in 1998 and in 2003 and noted, for example, a decrease in desire to read in 10- to 11-year-olds from 77 per cent to 65 per cent. In the Reading Champions survey (Clark *et al.* 2005), again reading attitudes are seen to decline with age and in the Nestlé Family Monitor research (2003), whilst most of the 11- to 18-year-olds report reading books in their spare time, girls again report reading more for pleasure than boys and a small but significant proportion believe reading does not play an important role in their lives. A third say they have better things to do than read books and a quarter suggest that they would be disappointed if someone gave them book.

Little media attention has been afforded these multiple data sources which indicate a distinct lack of pleasure in reading on the part of an increasing number of learners, although the English government did commission a survey to investigate reading for purpose and pleasure (Ofsted 2004). This reveals that many schools had given insufficient thought to promoting children's independent reading or building on children's textual preferences. Few schools successfully engaged the interests of those who, whilst competent readers, did not choose to read for pleasure and furthermore, in the less effective schools, additional support for strugglers focused on raising attainment, and did little to improve attitudes on the part of those who saw little point in reading. Whilst schools must take responsibility for their own actions, it must be acknowledged that from the inception of the literacy hour, it was predicted that reading for pleasure would take a step backwards. Meek (1998), Dombey (1998), Furlong (1998) and Burgess-Macey (1999) all warned there was limited encouragement of reading for pleasure in the National Literacy Strategy (NLS) (DfEE 1998), and in the prescribed literacy hour itself there was no mention of it. As Dombey (1998) observed, there was also almost no mention of purpose in literacy teaching and learning in the original documentation, although she acknowledged:

> Mention is made, at the end of a long list of technical competences, of enjoyment, evaluation, justification of preferences, imagination, inventiveness and critical awareness. But these appear, like a little-used list of desserts, detached from the menu that precedes them – to be enjoyed if at all only after pupils have eaten up all their nutritious technical cabbage. They are unlikely to flourish from strict application of the Framework.
>
> (Dombey 1998: 129–30)

Nine years later, whilst some schools and teachers have no doubt chosen to sustain a commitment to reading aloud and the promotion of literature and other reading materials, many others, in assiduously following the NLS, may well have reduced opportunities for voluntary/ independent reading for pleasure (Frater 2001; Martin 2003; Cremin et al. 2007). In concentrating on developing children's knowledge about particular linguistic, structural or lexical aspects of texts, it appears that the reason for reading the text in the first place may have been seriously neglected. As Philip Pullman observed, there were 71 verbs in the original NLS connected to the act of reading; 'enjoy' was not one of them (2003). In addition, concerns have been voiced about the fragmentation of the experience of reading, demonstrated through the use of decontextualized text extracts, the absence of meaningful interaction in shared reading (Burns and Myhill 2004) and reduced opportunities to enjoy texts at length (Fisher 2005; Gamble 2007). Professional authors too have voiced their consternation at the skills-based orientation of the NLS, and the focus on analysis and scrutiny of texts at the expense of pleasure and engagement (Powling et al. 2003).

The decline in reading for pleasure documented by Sainsbury and Schagen (2004) is seen to be related to the introduction of the NLS, although they acknowledge the complexity of this issue in the context of rapid technological advances and the changing nature of childhood. In addition, in a survey to understand the reduction in primary-phase book spending, Hurd *et al.* (2006: 85) conclude: 'There is evidence that reading is being neglected beyond the confines of the Literacy Hour and that schools no longer view reading across the school day as a priority.' The accumulating evidence suggests therefore that despite the gains in terms of reading attainment associated with the NLS (in 1998 65 per cent of 11-year-olds reached the target level in English; by 2005 nearly 80 per cent reached it), there have been losses, most notably in relation to children's attitudes to reading. As Steve Anwyll, the director of the Strategy, acknowledged in 2004:

> If we're increasing the attainment of children at the expense of their engagement and enjoyment, then we're failing to do the whole job and we have to take that seriously.
>
> (Hall 2004: 120)

Motivated to read?

To foster delight and pleasure in reading, surely increased attention needs to be paid to motivating readers and to the construction of creatively engaging environments which nurture children's personal encounters with literature and other texts and offer them choice, giving space and time to read voluntarily and share their preferences. There is also a real need to develop their intrinsic motivation 'in the form of a positive self-concept; a desire and tendency to read; and a reported enjoyment of an interest in reading' (Sainsbury and Schagen 2004: 374). Low achievers often have limited intrinsic motivation to read and indifferent or negative attitudes towards reading, and may see reading as a chore. Additionally perhaps, compounded by an extended period of failure and a reduced sense of self-efficacy, many appear to lack faith in their efforts (Pressley 1998). In the NLT survey, the young people believed they would read more if they enjoyed it more, had more time, if books were cheaper or about subjects they were interested in (Clark and Foster 2005).

As Woods outlines in the opening quote to this chapter, extrinsic motivation involves readers reading to satisfy the demands of others – to pass tests, to meet school or parents' expectations, for example. Wigfield and Guthrie (1997) identify three aspects of extrinsic motivation, namely: reading for recognition, for grades and for competition, so readers who are extrinsically motivated are not necessarily reading because they desire to do so or are interested in the subject matter. In contrast, readers who are intrinsically motivated are more likely to be reading for their own pleasure and satisfaction; studies suggest these readers may be reading more widely and more frequently and enjoying their reading more (Cox and Guthrie 2001). The aspects of intrinsic motivation identified by Wigfield and Guthrie (1997) which, according to their research, predict both reading breadth and comprehension include: importance, curiosity, involvement and a preference for challenge. It would appear then that keen independent readers believe reading is a worthwhile activity and continue to challenge themselves, reinforcing and developing their competence as readers in the process (for a more extended examination of reading motivation, see Guthrie and Wigfield 2000).

Reading for pleasure is thus closely related to intrinsic, not extrinsic motivation and when other variables have been accounted for, intrinsic motivation is positively correlated with reading comprehension (Cox and Guthrie 2001; Wang and Guthrie 2004). However, as Clark and Rumbold (2006) highlight, the relationship between intrinsic and extrinsic motivation is not a simple 'good versus evil' scenario, since children may well be motivated by both intrinsic and extrinsic aspects. They may read for their own pleasure and be obliged to read for others' purposes in school (Lepper and Henderlong 2000); furthermore, the reading repertoire needs to include all types of reading. Excessive extrinsic motivation and pressure to perform in school may drown a child's intrinsic desire to read, since, as Bernard Ashley observes: 'because children have to sweat so much over books, reading for recreation for some is like going for a leisure swim in their own dirty bathwater' (2003: 4).

Reading preferences

Over the last decades the nature and form of what children can choose to read has changed radically, partly as a consequence of rapid technological advances and the increasing dominance of the image. The multi-modal texts now readily available commonly include sound and music, voices, intonation, stance, gesture and movement, as well as print and image, and exist in different media such as computer screen, film, radio and book. 'These multi-modal texts have changed the ways in which young people expect to read, the ways they think and the ways they construct meaning' (Bearne 2003: 98).

Today's children bring to their reading considerable experience of reading and viewing texts of many kinds, and the NLT survey confirms that outside class children chose to read a very diverse range of texts. The most preferred reading materials reported upon by primary children in this study were: jokes (75 per cent), magazines (72 per cent), comics (69 per cent), fiction (62 per cent), TV books and magazines (61 per cent), signs (57 per cent), poetry (54 per cent) and websites (51 per cent). In the Nestlé Family Monitor (2003) survey, seven in ten of the young people said they would rather watch TV/DVD/video than read a book and over half reported a preference for using the internet over book reading. The recent UKLA Reading on Screen research (QCA/UKLA, forthcoming) also shows a rich variety of home-based text experience, both screen-based and on paper and a higher preference for multi-modal screen-based texts over those composed mainly of words in relation to leisure reading. It is worth noting though that in this research there was no lack of interest in sustained book reading at home; the children surveyed appeared to be aware that they could gain different reading satisfactions from different types of text. Additionally, these data suggest that reading on screen often boosts the reading of paper-based texts, with frequent indications of crossovers or links between screen texts and written texts. Fears and assumptions about the influence of popular cultural texts and TV competing with book reading still remain, but research evidence has shown that the processes involved in reading print and watching TV have similarities as well as differences (Robinson and Mackey 2003), that children's reading skills can be developed through reading film (Reid 2003; Blakemore 2006) and that moving image texts can enhance learners' motivation to engage in print related texts (Marsh and Millard 2000).

School provision

The culture of low book spending in Britain (Hurd *et al.* 2006) is in stark contrast to Norway, for example, where book spending per pupil is seven times higher (Howson 1999). Furthermore, the rich diversity of popular multi-modal texts is not fully reflected in the primary curriculum which, Marsh (2004) argues, relies on a canon of established and privileged texts and marginalizes popular culture and media texts – the very texts that received some of the highest ratings in terms of what children choose to read outside school. Ofsted (2004), too, note that schools rarely build on pupils' own reading interests or home materials.

Drawing on detailed ethnographic data collected in multi-ethnic communities in London, Gregory and Williams (2000: 164) also observe that there is a clear distinction between the reading matter that is enjoyed in the home and that which is sanctioned in school. This significant research additionally highlights the wealth of literacy practices in the lives of those often considered by the establishment to be deprived of literacy, revealing the breadth of formal learning and reading experienced outside school by children in multilingual families as well as the range of 'unofficial' reading matter found in monolingual families. Luke (1988) suggests that the reification of the 'residual tradition' of fairytales and approved authors in schools, shown, for example, in the 'significant children's authors' of the English National Curriculum (DfEE 1999), fails to recognize 'the emergent alternate tradition' and reduces the relevance of much reading material presented to young learners. It is encouraging, however, that the significantly renewed NLS (DfES 2006) does include a much greater awareness of Information and Communications Technology (ICT) and film texts and now refers to 'reading on page and on screen' recognizing a need to promote reading for pleasure. There is however no explicit mention of magazines and comics nor reference to producers or directors as authors. A culturally relevant range of texts and an accompanying culturally responsive pedagogy is arguably a necessity (Ladson-Billings 1995), not only to increase the possibility of making meanings and connections, but also to ensure that reading is not removed from its socio-cultural context.

> When pupils reject texts it may well not be because they do not understand them ... Having understood, they then reject the text on experiential grounds, on ideological grounds, on grounds of lack of emotional satisfaction: because, in my shorthand, they do not find themselves in it.
>
> (Sarland 1991: 101)

In relation to school provision, choice is critical; many studies show that when children select texts for themselves, this enhances their motivation and self-determination (Krashen 1993; Sanacore 1999). The work of Jeffrey and Woods (2003) highlights the role of agency, autonomy and ownership in creative learning and Gambrell (1996) indicates that when children are asked to comment on a book they have enjoyed, over 80 per cent mention one they chose for themselves. Choice is widely perceived to be a motivator, since interested and determined readers will often persist with a demanding text, simply because of their desire to know, to understand and to make sense of it. Yet Ofsted (2004) report that struggling readers are given less autonomy and choice in their reading and, as the UKLA response to the Rose Report notes, such readers are 'exposed to less text and have fewer and more limited opportunities to practise than more skilled peers' (2005: section

5). As a consequence they may be slower to become fluent, are less likely to find reading rewarding and may seek to avoid reading activities, perpetuating their sense of failure. Children with difficulties need support to enhance their motivation, engagement and self-esteem and need to be offered choices, albeit supported ones, from a range of potentially engaging texts. Tempting them to read relevant and interesting material may enable them to discover what reading can offer them as individuals.

Reading: meaning and purpose

Successful teachers of reading and literacy are, research suggests, not only knowledgeable about children's literature, they also prioritize the importance of meaning, not minutiae, and use whole texts for teaching and for sharing (Medwell *et al.* 1998). Significantly, they place great emphasis on 'children's recognition of the purposes and functions of reading and writing' (p.7). For, as Meek observes:

> Readers are made when they discover the activity is 'worth it'. Poor, inadequate, inexperienced readers lack literary competence because they have too little idea of what is 'in' reading for them.
>
> (Meek 1990: 76)

Reading for pleasure is oriented towards finding personal meaning and purpose and related to the human need to make sense of the world, the desire to understand, to make things work, to make connections, engage emotionally and feel deeply. In finding resonances in the text, whether inter-personal, extra-personal or inter-textual (Smith 2005), readers make meaning and turn such meanings over in their hands, their heads and their hearts. Owning a first book as a child, retaining a text which connects to a significant memory and lending/borrowing a book to/from a friend all reflect a function of the desire to read, indicate a degree of delight in reading itself and the need to share one's affective engagement. Beverley Naidoo (2003), in reflecting on the potency of recognizing ourselves in what we read, observed that Anne Frank's diary 'was the first book that made me realize that reading is real ... I still feel connected to her voice 40 years on – I still have my first copy – I could not part with it'. Young readers find different reasons for reading, but all deserve to encounter texts which have particular salience and interest to them, so that they can come to value the experience and be caught in a web of fiction or non-fiction which inspires and motivates them to return – to renew such an imaginatively energizing engagement. Benton and Fox (1985) highlight the emotional need to read and, in responding to questions about why they read, some children too assert that the affective dimension is a key motivator (Dungworth *et al.* 2004). Other studies indicate that children read because they see it as a life skill or perceive it will help them find out what they want/need to know (Clark and Foster 2005). A group of avid 10-year-old readers, discussing this question with their teacher, were asked to offer a statement each about why they read. They observed:

It makes me feel really alive.
You can lose yourself in another world.
I want to know all about my team.
I like to laugh and tell jokes.
I like being in a hot tub in my imagination.
I just get thirsty for stories.

Motivated and successful readers, these young people clearly find the personal and social processes of reading worthwhile. Their individual thirst for narrative, or for information about their football team, demonstrates that reading is connected in subtle but significant ways to these children's affective lives. One boy in the group, exasperated that Garth Nix and other fantasy authors insisted on producing series fiction commented, 'It makes it so difficult – I simply can't bear to wait and I wake up dreaming about what will happen and have to wait months to know all the time I'm desperate – it's not fair.' Yet he will wait and will persevere with other texts in the interim to satisfy his hunger for imaginative world creation.

In the more extended examples which follow, which were either observed by the writer or, in Robbie's case, shared with the writer, literacy is put to use in playful and open-ended contexts, by individuals or groups exerting a sense of their own agency and volition. In their different socio-cultural contexts, the salient issues of purpose and pleasure are evidenced by each of the readers, whose desire to read and think about possible meanings is fuelled by previous experiences of delight and a deep sense of satisfaction in reading itself.

Reading as playful engagement

Despite being encased in plaster from her armpits down to her toes, with an iron rod separating her legs to prevent movement, Sarah, nearly 26 months old, drags herself determinedly across the floor to where a pile of well-worn books lie. Pushing herself almost upright, she decimates the pile, apparently searching for one particular text. Once *Where's My Teddy?* by Jez Alborough (1993) comes into view, she smiles broadly and seizes it with delight, almost hugging it to her. Then, squawking loudly, she draws her mother's attention, makes her meaning clear and awaits the rhyming tale with anticipation. Helen has clearly read it so often that she has begun to remember the words and reads with a performed aplomb. Throughout, Sarah nods her head from side to side, her eyes alight, especially when the great big bear arrives. She responds to her mother's informal comments and questions by pointing, gesturing and making noises and when the hero Eddie is finally reunited with his own bear Sarah claps her hands and sets off again across the floor to collect a tiny teddy lying under a chair. On her return her mother rereads the page and Sarah, still flat on her stomach, acts out the role of the protagonist, cuddling her teddy and making whispering noises in his ear. As the end paper is reached, she quickly turns the book over and looks up at her mother expectantly. When the second reading of the book comes to a close, Sarah and her mother cuddle the bear together and Helen, extending the narrative, begins a one-sided conversation with the teddy, asking about the big bear and telling him in hushed tones how glad she is to have him home. Later when Sarah goes for a nap she insists on being read the book again and takes the tiny bear with her, as indeed Eddie took his own teddy to bed at the end of the story.

This brief textual encounter demonstrates not only the imaginative potency of this tale to Sarah, but also the pleasure, intimacy and physicality of this reading partnership. Despite her inability to move freely, she still took part in bringing the text to life, taking particular delight in the patterns and rhythms that connect to the nursery rhymes and church choruses which are an established part of her early literacy life. As Meek (1988) has demonstrated, what children read plays a vital role in their anticipation of pleasure and success, even before their ability to read for themselves. Through her mother's interchanges and actions, both during the reading and afterwards, Sarah was learning to engage with and interpret the narrative and was evidently enjoying the experience. Reading, Britton (1982) suggests, is built on a legacy of past satisfactions and whilst such satisfactions cannot be guaranteed as this young child grows, the deep pleasure of such early reading encounters provide her with firm foundations.

Reading as life-coping

The next example, whilst not seeking to endorse what the US entitle 'bibliotherapy', does reflect the degree of emotional support that reading can offer and highlights the significance of teachers' judgements based on their knowledge of learners and of literature. Eileen, a teaching colleague, heard her tutor struggle to read the demanding picture book *Jenny Angel* by Margaret Wild (her tutor had lost a god-daughter and it evoked painful memories) and immediately afterwards insisted on taking the book home with her – a child in her class had need of it. It tells the tale of Jenny who wants to be an angel for her brother Davy who is dying. She finds she cannot save him and the book, powerfully illustrated by Anne Spudvilas, explores her feelings and ability to cope. It is somehow both uplifting and sustaining, in a manner not dissimilar to the better known *Grandpa* by John Burningham (1984). Eileen read it to Robbie, a 6-year-old whose mother was ill, in the hope that it might offer some shape and substance for his feelings, and later, at his mother's request, it was lent to the family. It was read and discussed and Robbie was apparently often seen poring over the pages by himself. Several weeks later, of his own volition, he produced his own version (see Figures 10.1–10.5).

Robbie's imaginative transformation of the narrative, underpinned by a deep emotional purpose, is poignantly expressed in this creative reconstruction, in which he appears to offer himself an imaginative lifeline, becoming both the teller and the told. He powerfully conveys the happiness of his characters, as reunited they play on the 'climbing frame shaped like a heart'. His tale too was apparently read and reread and kept with the original book – as a kind of life-coping companion perhaps. His text, and the context which enabled it, demonstrate again that reading is not only a cognitive, but an emotional, aesthetic and ethical act. It also demonstrates the significance of teachers' sensitive judgements, their close attention to individual emergent and diverse identities and to the social context and personal and cultural resources upon which children draw. Teachers cannot mandate young people's deep engagement in the world of literature, but they can and should know their learners and the world of children's literature well enough to make connections and recommend texts which variously offer solace, sustenance, support and challenge.

Reading as critical reflection

It is independent reading time in a class of 9- to 10-year-olds and an air of focused activity pervades the scene. Children are scattered in pairs and groups around the room, talking, laughing, reading and sharing texts of various kinds. One group, lounging on cushions in the book area, are seemingly intent on their novels. Occasionally they shift their physical positions but otherwise remain focused, experiencing life vicariously, as they inhabit the 'secret garden of the novel – that special sanctuary'

Figure 10.1:   Jenny Angel 2.

Figure 10.2: Jenny was walking to the park by the church and saw Davy in the churchyard. She ran over to him.

Davys heart was
Still Beating
geting fastar and
fastar and Broke
outi He climbed
outof the ground.

Figure 10.3: Davy's heart was still beating, getting faster and faster, and broke out. He climbed out of the ground.

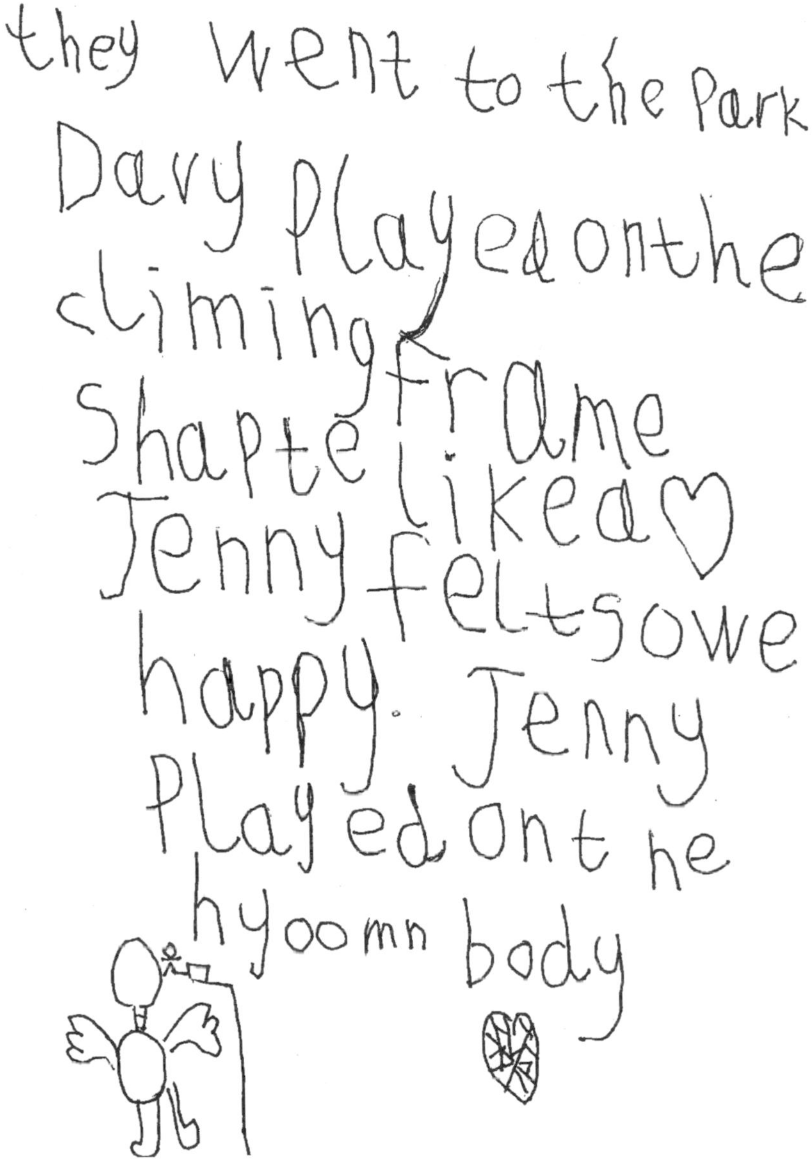

Figure 10.4: They went to the park. Davy played on the climbing frame shaped like a heart. Jenny felt so very happy. Jenny played on the human body.

they went very fast
to Maries huose
and playedand
Played until dinner
time

ThoEnd

Figure 10.5: They went very fast to Marie's house and played and played until dinner time. The end.

(Doherty 2001). Another group pore over the pages of self-chosen non-fiction texts, some, individually selected from the library, are about quad bikes and astronauts, whilst others relate to the class focus on the environment. On one table, comics are spread in colourful splendour and children scrutinize the pages of the *Beano* and the *Dandy* with evident pleasure, occasionally sharing elements of interest and amusement. At the two computers, pairs of learners surf the net, talking rapidly as they search for sites of interest – eventually one pair settle on the Tracey Beaker site, while the others move around sites relating to dangerous creatures. This pair seeks permission to print off some of the images and set up a file to save highlights of the information encountered. Another group is gathered around a box of picture fiction and poetry which has been jointly constructed by members of the staff and this class bringing in childhood favourites to share. The embossed book plates in the end papers are examined constantly to see whose book it is and much discussion is generated about this issue, even before the books are sampled. The teacher is sitting with the last group – a guided reading group – examining a collection of contemporary children's magazines, including *Smash Hits*, *Girl Talk*, *Match!* and *Mizz*. Again it transpires that whilst some of these have been purchased, many have been donated by the children – increasing the range available and honouring their home reading.

In this group, the teacher, seeking to help the children enjoy and interrogate what they read, allocates time to browsing and informal interactions before focusing first on the front covers and then on a particular article on fashion. During the last activity the children pose various questions including:

> Why choose these people?
> Why set it out this way?
> Did they ask the stars to wear them on purpose?
> Did they all get coats or just them?
> Do the girls like the style of coats?
> Did Jane actually say that?
>
> > (Swain 2005: 39)

The group were learning to read against the text, and were developing a critical awareness that texts represent particular points of view and often silence other perspectives (Comber and Simpson 2001). At the close of reading time, the class were invited to offer information, extracts or comments on what they had been reading. Their willingness to share their thoughts and enthusiasm for authors, websites and comic strip heroes as well as their criticism of particular staff choices and texts was marked. In this class, reading, discussing and questioning texts was seen as the norm, and the children's choices and voices were recognized and honoured as integral to promoting reading for pleasure, engagement and critical reflection.

Creative practice

In the Rose Review, best practice in teaching reading is described as formalized in design, but taught creatively with due regard for individual differences (Rose 2006). Yet the two-dimensional conceptual framework advocated in the Rose Review, the 'simple view of reading' that separates decoding and comprehension, has the potential, if not carefully handled, to focus the attention of teachers and young readers on words not meanings, sounds not sense. A potentially piecemeal approach, it may short-change children's pleasure in reading still further. Surely an equally simple view is that the early reading curriculum should focus first and foremost on enabling children to develop a range of strategies in order to become competent and enthusiastic readers, who can and do choose to read for pleasure and enjoyment.

As teachers seek to respond to the requirement to privilege synthetic phonics and to separate word recognition and comprehension, creativity will undoubtedly be needed to ensure that enticing invitations to inhabit and explore potent texts from the inside out are still offered and positive attitudes are actively developed. Through constructing creative contexts in which relevant reading is encountered for personal purposes, parents, carers and teachers can invite learners to engage in the active process of meaning making and encourage them to reflect critically on texts and learn from them. Such invitations to engage, personally, emotionally and cognitively, have the potential to increase learners' confidence and desire to read and to heighten their motivation. Additionally, teachers conscious of other core strands of creative pedagogic practice will plan to nurture the agency of young readers, foster their curiosity and offer them choice from a range of multi-modal texts connected to their interests and their lives. Time for discussion and collaboration will also be offered as well as a rich diet of reading aloud and a range of book promotion activities that enable children to share their preferences and widen their possibilities in a community of engaged readers. Reflecting upon reading will thread through such creative practice that profiles meaning and purpose, pleasure and play.

Explicit literacy teaching is at times both useful and necessary, but as the degree of explicitness increases, the aesthetic space for learners decreases and so, in routinizing textual encounters and focusing on comprehension only after word recognition has been mastered, teachers may reduce the gaps that exist for the learner to become affectively involved and make connections. Creative teachers appear to exploit the potential spaces, problems and possibilities which literature offers, recognizing that the silences or gaps in texts (Iser 1978) increase the uncertainty and thus the potential for personal engagement, prompting generative discussion. Good book talk, which is essential for developing readers' understandings of the multilayered and emergent meanings of texts (Chambers 1993), can be a powerful motivator since it involves honouring the children's own creative responses, their questions, connections and thoughts. In a pedagogy which focuses on reading, not criticism (Benton and Fox 1985), fluid and open interpretations of texts are fostered, which may later relate to considering how the writer elicited such responses. Creatively teaching reading, practitioners will not focus merely on children learning to read and write, a minimum entitlement, but will focus on 'teaching for the maximum entitlement – to become a reader for life' (Martin 2003: 14).

Conclusion

Regardless of any recommended changes in reading instruction, developing children's desire to read for pleasure remains a key priority for the primary profession if a further decline is to be avoided. Teachers need to offer a coherent and creative literacy curriculum that develops children's intrinsic motivation to read, creates an engaging physical and social environment for reading, provides pupil choice and encompasses diversity as well as focused instruction and tailored support. In the process, full attention must be paid to meaning and purpose, the details of text reception, the social context, values, attitudes and culture in the class, the school and the community. In explicitly planning to nurture positive attitudes, teachers will need to respond to children's interests, offer a diverse range of potent texts and engage them in the selection process, seeking in addition to strengthen home–school–community partnerships and enable creative engagement through enriched pedagogical practice. In creating a reading culture which fuels delight and fosters desire, teachers will be supporting the development of lifelong readers, readers who find both purpose and pleasure in reading.

References

Aarnoutse, C. and Van Leeuwe, J. (1998) Relation between reading comprehension, vocabulary, reading pleasure and reading frequency, *Educational Research and Evaluation*, 4: 143–66.

Alborough, J. (1993) *Where's my Teddy?* London: Walker Books.

Ashley, B. (2003) Books in school, in C. Powling, B. Ashley, P. Pullman, A. Fine and J. Gavin (eds) *Meetings with the Minister*. Reading: National Centre for Language and Literacy.

Bearne, E. (2003) Rethinking literacy: communication, representation and text, *Reading Literacy and Language*, 37 (3): 98–103.

Benton, M. and Fox, R. (1985) *Teaching Literature 9–14*. Oxford: Oxford University Press.

Burningham, J. (1984) *Grandpa*. London: Jonathon Cape.

Blakemore, L. (2006) Reading and Film: Exploring Connections. Unpublished MA dissertation, Canterbury Christ Church University.

Britton, J. (1982) *Prospect and Retrospect: Selected Essays of James Britton*, edited by G. Pradl. London: Heinemann.

Burgess-Macey, C. (1999) Classroom literacies: young children's explorations in meaning making in the age of the literacy hour, *Reading*, 33 (3): 120–5.

Burns, C. and Myhill, D. (2004) Interactive or inactive? A consideration of the nature of interaction in whole class teaching', *Cambridge Journal of Education*, 34 (3): 35–49.

Chambers, A. (1993) *Tell Me: Children, Reading and Talk*. Stroud: Thimble Press.

Clark, C. and Foster, A. (2005) *Children's and Young People's Reading Habits and Preferences: The Who, What, Why, Where and When*. London: National Literacy Trust.

Clark, C. and Rumbold, K. (2006) *Reading for Pleasure: A Research Overview*. London: National Literacy Trust.

Clark, C., Torsi, S. and Strong, J. (2005) *Young People and Reading*. London: National Literacy Trust.

Comber, B. and Simpson, A. (eds) (2001) *Negotiating Critical Literacies in Classrooms*. Mahwah, NJ and London: Lawrence Erlbaum Associates.

Cox, K.E. and Guthrie, J.T. (2001) Motivational and cognitive contributions to students' amount of reading, *Contemporary Educational Psychology*, 26 (1): 116–31.

Cremin, T., Bearne, E. Goodwin, P. and Mottram, M. (2007) Teachers reading in the 21st century, Paper given at Acts of Reading Conference, 19–20 April, Cambridge University.

Cunningham, A.E. and Stanovich, K.E. (1998) What reading does for the mind, *American Educator*, 22 (1&2): 8–15.

DfEE (Department for Education and Employment) (1998) *The National Literacy Strategy Framework for Teaching*. London: DfEE.

DfEE (1999) *The National Curriculum: Handbook for Primary Teachers in England*. London: HMSO.

DfES (Department for Education and Skills) (2003) *Excellence and Enjoyment: A Strategy for Primary Schools*. Nottingham: DfES.

DfES (2004) *Every Child Matters: Change for Children* (DfES-1110-2004). The Stationery Office.

DfES (2006) *Framework for Teaching Mathematics and Literacy*. London: The Stationery Office.

Doherty, B. (2001) Recognising yourself in what you read, Keynote speech at 'Just let me think: reflecting on literacy learning', United Kingdom Reading Association International Conference, 6–8 July, Canterbury.

Dombey, H. (1998) Changing literacy in the early years of school, in B. Cox (ed.) *Literacy is not Enough: Essays on the Importance of Reading*. Manchester: Manchester University Press and Book Trust.

Dungworth, N., Grimshaw, S., McKnight, C. and Morris, A. (2004) Reading for pleasure? A summary of the findings from a survey of the reading habits of Year 5 pupils, *New Review of Children's Literature and Librarianship*, 10: 169–88.

Fisher, R. (2005) Teacher–child interaction in the teaching of reading: a review of research perspectives over twenty five years, *Journal of Research in Reading*, 28 (1): 15–27.

Frater, G. (2001) *Effective Practice in Writing at Key Stage 2*. London: The Basic Skills Agency.

Furlong, T. (1998) Reading in the primary school, in B. Cox (ed.) *Literacy is Not Enough. Essays on the Importance of Reading*. Manchester: Manchester University Press and Book Trust.

Gamble, N. (2007) Teaching literature in T. Cremin and H. Dombey, *Handbook on the Teaching of Primary English in Initial Teacher Education*. London: UKLA/NATE.

Gambrell, L.B. (1996) Creating classroom cultures that foster reading motivation, *The Reading Teacher*, 50: 14–25.

Gregory, E. and Williams, A. (2000) *City Literacies*. London: Routledge-Falmer.

Guthrie, J.T. and Alvermann, D. E. (1999) *Engaged Reading: Processes, Practices, and Policy Implications*. New York: Teachers College Press.

Guthrie, J.T. and Wigfield, A. (2000) Engagement and motivation in reading, in C. Hall and M. Coles (1999) *Children's Reading Choices*. London: Routledge Falmer.

Hall, K. (2004) Reflecting on six years of the National Literacy Strategy in England: an interview with Stephen Anwyll, Director NLS 2001–04, *Literacy*, 38 (1): 19–25.

Howson, J. (1999) Have schools got the book balance right?, *Times Educational Supplement*, 2 July.

Hurd, S., Dixon, M. and Oldham, J. (2006) Are low levels of book spending in primary schools jeopardising the National Literacy Strategy?, *The Curriculum Journal*, 17 (1): 73–88.

Iser, W. (1978) *The Act of Reading*, Baltimore, MD: Johns Hopkins University Press.

Jeffrey, B. and Woods, P. (2003) *The Creative School: A Framework for Success, Quality and Effectiveness*. London: RoutledgeFalmer.

Krashen, S. (1993) *The Power of Reading*. Englewood, DC: Libraries Unlimited, Inc

Ladson-Billings, G. (1995) Towards a theory of culturally relevant pedagogy *American Educational Research Journal*, 32 (3): 465–91.

Lepper, M.R. and Henderlong, J. (2000) Turning 'play' into 'work' and 'work' into 'play': 25 years of research on intrinsic and extrinsic motivation, in C. Sansone and J.M. Harackiewicz (eds) *Intrinsic and Extrinsic Motivation: The Search for Optimal Motivation and Performance*. San Diego, CA: Academic Press.

Luke, A. (1988) *Literacy, Textbooks and Ideology: Postwar Literacy Instruction and the Mythology of Dick and Jane*. London: Falmer.

Marsh, J. (2004) The techno-literacy practices of young children, *Journal of Early Childhood Research*, 2 (1): 51–6.

Marsh, J. and Millard, E. (eds) (2000) *Popular Literacies, Childhood and Schooling*. London: Routledge.

Martin, T. (2003) Minimum and maximum entitlements: literature at key stage 2, *Reading Literacy and Language*, 37 (1): 14–17.

Medwell, J., Wray, D., Poulson, L. and Fox, R. (1998) *Effective Teachers of Literacy: A Report of a Research Project Commissioned by the Teacher Training Agency*. Exeter: University of Exeter.

Meek, M. (1988) *How Texts Teach What Readers Learn*. Stroud: Thimble Press.

Meek, M. (1990) Why response?, in M. Hayhoe and S. Parker (eds) *Reading and Response*. Buckingham: Open University Press.

Meek, M. (1998) Important reading lessons, in B. Cox (ed.) *Literacy is Not Enough. Essays on the Importance of Reading*. Manchester: Manchester University Press and Book Trust.

Mullis, I.V.S., Martin, M.O., Gonzalez, E.J. and Kennedy, A.M. (2003) *PIRLS 2001 International Report: IEA's Study of Reading Literacy Achievement in Primary Schools*. Chestnut Hill, MA: Boston College.

Naidoo, B. (2003) Out of bounds, Keynote speech at United Kingdom Reading Association International Conference, 8–10 July, Cambridge.

Nestlé Family Monitor (2003) *Young People's Attitudes Towards Reading*. Croydon: Nestlé.

OECD (2002) *Reading for Change: Performance and Engagement Across Countries: Results from PISA 2002*. New York: Organization for Economic Cooperation and Development.

Ofsted (2004) *Reading for Purpose and Pleasure: An Evaluation of the Teaching of Reading in Primary Schools*. London: Ofsted.

Powling, C., Ashley, B., Pullman, P., Fine, A. and Gavin, J. (2003) *Meetings with the Minister: Five Children's Authors on the National Literacy Strategy*. Reading: National Centre for Language and Literacy.

Pressley, M. (1998) *Reading Instruction that Works: The Case for Balanced Reading*. New York: Guildford Press.

Pullman, P. (2003) Teaching and testing, in C. Powling, B. Ashley, P. Pullman, A. Fine and J. Gavin (eds) *Meetings with the Minister*. Reading: National Centre for Language and Literacy.

QCA/UKLA (forthcoming): *Reading on Screen: Research Undertaken by UKLA with Support from QCA*. London: Qualifications and Curriculum Authority.

Reid, M. (2003) Writing film: making inferences when viewing and reading, *Literacy*, 37 (3): 111–15.

Robinson, M. and Mackey, M. (2003) Film and television in N. Hall, J. Larson and J. Marsh (eds) *Handbook of Early Childhood Literacy*. London, New Delhi, Thousand Oaks, CA: Sage Publications.

Rose (2006) *An Independent Review of the Teaching of Early Reading*. Nottingham: DfES.

Sainsbury, M. and Schagen, I. (2004) Attitudes to reading at ages nine and eleven. *Journal of Research in Reading*, 27: 373–86.

Sanacore, J. (1999) Encouraging children to make choices about their literacy Learning, *Intervention in School and Clinic*, 35: 38–42.

Sarland, C. (1991) *Young People Reading: Culture and Response*. Milton Keynes: Open University Press.

Smith, V. (2005) *Making Reading Mean*. Leicester: UKLA.

Swain, C. (2005) Critical Readings: If You Don't Question What You Read, Then What's the Point in Reading? Unpublished MA dissertation, Canterbury Christ Church University College.

Topping, K. Valtin, R. Roller, C. Brozo, W. and Lourdes Dionsiso, M. (2003) *Policy and Practice Implication of PISA 2000: Report of the PISA Task Force to the International Reading Association Board of Directors*. New York: International Reading Association.

Twist, L. *et al.* (2003) *Reading All Over the World: PIRLS National Report for England*. Slough: National Foundation for Educational Research/ DfES.

UKLA (United Kingdom Literacy Association) (2005) *Submission to the Rose Review*. Accessed online at: http://www.ukla.org, July 2006.

Wang, J.H.Y. and Guthrie, J.T. (2004) Modeling the effects of intrinsic motivation, extrinsic motivation, amount of reading, and past reading achievement on text comprehension between US and Chinese students, *Reading Research Quarterly*, 39: 162–86.

Whitehead, F. (1977) *Children and Their Books*. London: Macmillan.

Wigfield, A. and Guthrie, J. T. (1997) Relations of children's motivation for reading to the amount and breadth of their reading, *Journal of Educational Psychology*, 89: 420–32.

Wild, M. and Spudvilas, A. (1999) *Jenny Angel*. Australia: Penguin.

Woods, P. (1995) *Creative Teachers in Primary Schools*. Buckingham: Open University Press.

Woods, P. (2001) Creative literacy, in A. Craft, B. Jeffrey and M. Liebling (eds) *Creativity in Education*. London: Continuum.

Index

LISTENING TO STEPHEN READ
Multiple Perspectives on Literacy

Kathy Hall

- How do different reading experts interpret evidence about one child as a reader?
- What perspectives can be brought to bear on reading in the classroom?
- How can a rich notion of literacy be promoted in the regular primary classroom?

In this book Kathy Hall invites you to extend your perspective on reading by considering the responses of well known reading scholars (e.g. Barbara Comber, Henrietta Dombey, Laura Huxford and David Wray) to one child as a reader.

Reading evidence from eight-year-old Stephen, who is 'under-achieving' in reading, together with the suggestions of various experts about how his teacher could support him provide a vehicle for discussing different perspectives on reading in the primary classroom. The various approaches to literacy analysed include psycho-linguistic, cognitive-psychological, socio-cultural and socio-political.

The book aims to guide your choice of teaching strategies and to support your rationale for those choices. Acknowledging the complexity and the richness of the field of research on literacy, the book demonstrates the futility of searching for a single right method of literacy development. Rather we should search for multiple perspectives, guided by the diverse needs of learners.

*Contents: **Part one: A psycho-linguistic perspective** – Ann Browne's observations, suggestions and theoretical perspectives – Teresa Grainger's observations, suggestions and theoretical perspectives – Reading as a problem-solving activity – **Part two: A cognitive-psychological perspective** – Laura Huxford's observations, suggestions and theoretical perspectives – David Wray's observations, suggestions and theoretical perspectives – Words matter – **Part three: A socio-cultural perspective** – Henrietta Dombey's observations, suggestions and theoretical perspectives – Mary Hilton's observations, suggestions and theoretical perspectives – Reading and communities of practice – **Part four: A socio-political perspective** – Barbara Comber's observations, suggestions and theoretical perspectives – Jackie Marsh's observations, suggestions and theoretical perspectives – Reading the word and the world – Conclusion*

2002   224pp
978-0-335-20758-9 (Paperback)